Write. Market. Succeed.
An Author's Marketing Playbook

A Step-By-Step Guide for How to Market You & Your Book for Success for Aspiring and Published Authors

Nicolette Lemmon

Copyright © 2023 Nicolette Lemmon

All rights reserved.

Printed in the United States of America

Disclaimer

The information and viewpoints in this book are those of Nicolette Lemmon. As the owner of a marketing agency for over 35 years, the intention of this marketing handbook is to share key marketing processes and ideas to enable authors to successfully promote and sell their book(s).

During the writing and editing of this handbook, every attempt has been made to verify the information, examples and customer stories provided to illustrate ways to effectively create author marketing. Neither the author nor the publisher assumes any responsibility for errors, omissions, or contrary interpretations of the subject matter herein. The views expressed are based on the author's personal experiences within the corporate world, education, and everyday life.

This book is for guiding authors in their understanding of marketing only. The views expressed are those of the author alone and should not be taken as expert instruction or commands. The reader is responsible for his or her future action. This book makes no guarantees of future success. However, by following the steps that are listed in this book, the ability to market your book(s) successfully has a much higher probability. Neither the author nor the publisher assumes any responsibility or liability on behalf of the purchaser or reader of these materials.

ISBN: 978-0-9650880-4-6

CONTENTS

Introduction 1
    A Quick Story!

Chapter 1 3
    Getting Started – Is Writing a Business or Hobby

Chapter 2 7
    Start by Defining Your Goals

Chapter 3 11
    The Author Brand to Support Your Writing Dream

Chapter 4 15
    Building Your Author Success Plan

Chapter 5 29
    Getting Started on Your Marketing Plan

Chapter 6 35
    Your Marketing Tool Chest

Chapter 7 45
    Your Promotional Campaign for Book Sales

Chapter 8 53
    Promoting Your Book from the Stage

Chapter 9 61
    Content Marketing Tips to Build Your Outreach

Chapter 10 71
    Positioning Yourself for Ongoing Success

Chapter 11 77
    20-Minute Author Marketing Audit

Chapter 12 81
    Help with Next Steps

Bonus: 93
    The Ease of Using Artificial Intelligence (AI)

About the Author 97

Acknowledgements 99

Bibliography 101

INTRODUCTION
A Quick Story!

Why were you attracted to this workbook? Whether you aspire to be published or are already a published author, if your idea of success is selling hundreds or thousands of books with adoring readers, and watching money roll in, it boils down to understanding the business of writing. While you must write a great fiction novel or non-fiction book, after writing is a profession and a business, there is one critical element: Marketing.

Years ago, I joined a group for mystery writers and was excited to meet other members. When I sat down at a table, one man introduced himself and handed me a flyer about his book. I asked how many he had sold so far, and he answered, "about 100." Another author introduced herself and handed me a printed bookmark that had her book cover and description on it. To others at the table, I asked how many books each had written as well as how many had been sold.

> **Writing a book and not promoting it is like having a baby and leaving it o a doorstep.**
>
> **Jack Canfield[1]**
> **National best-selling author and coach**

Then, the nosy marketer side of me asked what they were doing to sell more books. For example, how many people were on their email lists.

All looked at me like deer in headlights.

As the owner of a marketing firm for decades, it was clear these authors as well as other aspiring authors, self-published or traditionally published authors, most often have no clue about marketing. Some writers come from backgrounds in government, education, medicine, or other careers where they were never exposed to the elements of marketing. Most believed that a publisher would market their book.

Here are three things I learned from stepping into the writer's world:

First, many writers/authors are not comfortable with marketing because they do not know where to start or know little about the process and strategies. **Second**, if an author is traditionally published or seeking to be, they believe the publisher will do all the marketing. **Third**, most writers are not prepared to fund, or expect to fund, marketing and advertising to generate book sales.

According to an article by Berrett-Koehler Publishers[2], most book marketing today is done by authors, not by publishers. And according to Publishers Weekly, the average book in the United States has sold less than 200 copies per year and fewer than 1,000 copies in its lifetime.[3] In addition, Amazon has made it easier than ever to upload a manuscript as an e-book. The numbers have escalated to over twelve million eBooks on Amazon[4] with *millions* more uploaded every year.

With millions of eBooks available in the marketplace, there is also a huge backlog of existing books to add to the mix. That means there is incredible competition for a reader's attention. Whether traditionally or independently published, to sell books, you need to create an author brand and platform to engage readers and fans – an Author Success Plan.

From my long career in running a marketing agency and presenting workshops in a variety of industries, I found myself helping friends in writing groups to better understand how to promote their books.

In recent years I have presented writers workshops and tailored my marketing expertise into quick start strategy, tools, and tips for author branding and book sales. Several authors requested a workbook, so I tailored this handbook to help authors, regardless of their backgrounds, with a step-by-step process to promote and sell more books. Having often been asked for a workbook, I pulled together this one to support the busy writer who needs a jumpstart for their marketing.

The following pages offer an easy guide to treating writing as a business and the books are your products you create. Check out the "3 Action Steps" at the end of each chapter to help you move forward to build your book marketing. If you follow the guidance in this handbook, and complete the action steps, you will have a marketing plan that will propel sales.

The key is to use the ideas in this handbook to work their magic for your success.

CHAPTER 1
Getting Started – Is Writing a Business or Hobby

Choosing Your Path

Do you consider writing a business or a hobby? If you are not clear, here is a quiz to find out:

1. Are you writing to get a fiction novel or non-fiction book published?

2. Is getting your story or message read by lots of people the main goal?

3. Do you want to make money from your writing?

4. Do you regularly take courses, attend webinars, listen to podcasts, and read newsletters to sharpen your writing skills?

5. Do you want to be traditionally published?

6. Are you looking to independently publish on Amazon or another indie platform?

> If you don't know where you are going, any road will get you there.
>
> Lewis Carroll,
>
> *Alice in Wonderland*[5]

If you answered "YES" to 4 or more of the above questions, you have indicated you want more from your writing than merely to have it sit on your computer.

If you are striving to get your stories or expertise into the world, you are acting more like a businessperson than a hobbyist.

It is important to determine your motivation for writing. Over the last several years, Amazon has made it easier than ever to upload a manuscript as an eBook. Therefore, the hobbyist can upload an eBook and give family and friends a place to buy it.

If you are an author who wants to earn money by selling lots of your books, you are considering it a business. Every business requires marketing to sell its products or services, and the same applies to selling books. Marketing is a critical skillset to your writing business success.

A study suggests that of the millions of books carried in Barnes and Noble stores, less than 20% sell more than 1,000 copies. The Pareto Rule of 80/20 holds true with only 20% of the traditionally published authors selling more than 2,000 copies. Even the average indie published author makes around $1,000 per year according to The Guardian[6]. That's including many authors who have multiple books and a huge list of fans. In fact, nearly a third of the indie published authors made less than $500 a year and 90% of books sold less than 100 copies.[6]

The key to achieving more success is an Author Success Plan and consistent, ongoing marketing. Those best-selling authors who make six figures spend their time, talent, and treasure to achieve remarkable results. One of my writer friends has earned over half a million dollars as an indie author and she spends an hour per day on her book marketing.

It is achievable to have success in your writing business with focus and a plan.

You, as a Business

With many writers, the idea of crafting an amazing story is the initial focus. Once the manuscript is traditionally or indie published, writers often assume that their part is done. As mentioned in the introduction, often new authors are clueless about how to generate more sales and lack business/marketing knowledge.

Quick Checklist: Marketing Mindset for Authors

It takes a long time to write a fiction novel or nonfiction book, so start setting yourself up for success while you do!

First – Are you treating yourself as a business?
- ☐ You have a product (your writing) – Develop a description of your writing biz.
- ☐ You want income (via selling books) – Start a simple plan and budget.
- ☐ Be ready to promote your work – Take stock of your time, talent, and treasure.

Second – Identify your reader target and what will attract them to your book(s)
- ☐ Who reads your genre? Describe age, gender, employment, hobbies.
- ☐ Which other authors are similar to your work? Identify "like" reads.
- ☐ Why are your stories worth reading? Define the benefit for a reader.
- ☐ If published, does the back of your book description connect to that benefit?
- ☐ If aspiring, write up the back cover description with that benefit.

Third– Build A Success Network and Work Smart Structure
- ☐ Connect with other authors – Share email lists to promote each other's work.
- ☐ Be consistent with content – One piece can be repurposed in email, social media, and website.
- ☐ Stay visible – Choose monthly and weekly marketing touches. These can be scheduled emails, social media posts, advertising, conferences, and other ways to "touch" your target reader.

3 ACTION STEPS:

1. Make the decision if you are a hobbyist or a business owner? Which one fits your writing dream?

2. For the choice of making your writing a hobby or business, write a statement of what it will look like when you publish your book. Include how many books you want to sell, how many readers to join your email list, and a starter amount you can budget to get the book to market. Start with "When my book is published, I will feel successful when _____. [Examples: From book sales/royalties, I make back all the costs of writing, publishing, and marketing. I will feel successful when my book sales reach 1,000. I will feel successful once my royalties exceed my advance and I start receiving royalty checks. I will feel successful when I earn enough money from my book sales to quit my day job.]

3. To be clear, if you want to earn money from the sale of your book(s), today's competitive marketplace requires that you have a business focus. The starting point is to understand what you need to learn more about. On a scale of 1-10, where 1 is "little" and 10 is "proficient:"

   a. What is your level of knowledge with business planning?

   b. What is your level of experience with marketing?

Notes:

CHAPTER 2
Start by Defining Your Goals

The Concept of Goals

People use goals to focus on finishing projects, achieving dreams, and keeping life on track. The most important goal as a writer is to make the time to write.

Having the commitment with goals to working on your projects, in essence, provides the diligence to produce the best story and manuscript possible. And, setting goals helps with all projects, to get them completed using your time, talent, and treasure.

For your writing biz, as with any business, setting goals gives direction and motivation to increase the sales of your products each year. As a writer, you need to add business related goals to your writing ones, if you want to make money from book sales.

Setting and Tracking Your Goals

The key is to begin with your biggest goals for the completion of your writing projects to see how these will line up for the year. Without moving forward on your writing, you will not have anything to promote and sell. Then, break down the goals to monthly and weekly, even daily, to keep them top of mind and be realistic on what you can effectively achieve.

First, here is an example to organize your daily word count goal. This word count worksheet makes it easier to track your writing goals.

	Writing Challenge	# Words Beginning	# Words End of Day	Daily Novel Word Count	Cumulative Novel Word Count	Novel Average Pgs/Day this month	Additional Writing #1 Word Count	Additional Writing #2 Word Count	Additional Writing #3 Word Count	Journal Word Count	Total All Daily Writing Word Count	Cumulative All Writing Word Count	All Writing Average Pgs/Day
2	Project or Book Name												
3	MONTH												
4	1	0	1,100	1,100	1,100	1,100					1,100	1,100	1,100
5	2	1,100	1,500	400	1,500	750					400	1,500	750
6	3	1,500		0	1,500	500					0	1,500	500
7	4	0		0	1,500	375					0	1,500	375
8	5	0		0	1,500	300					0	1,500	300
9	6	0		0	1,500	250					0	1,500	250
10	7	0		0	1,500	214					0	1,500	56
11	8	0		0	1,500	188					0	1,500	188

Here is how I set up my tracking document. If tracking from the first of the month for a new project, put the daily word count in the first line in the yellow box. If you are comfortable using Excel or similar program, you can create a formula to have the word count populate for the next day in the column for "# Words Beginning." Or you can always just copy and paste the number. I also like to have additional columns for other writing that is not specific to the work in progress (WIP), yet I want to capture the time I spend writing overall. Using a color like in the yellow columns, the key is to enter the actual word count you wrote in the yellow boxes. Simple tracking helps to keep you focused.

For the month, create a formula to determine the average number of words per day by using the number of days you wrote divided into the overall word count. If computer spreadsheets are not tools you are comfortable using, you can achieve the same results with creatomg a table like the following sample worksheet.

Word Count# Tracking	Words# Beginning	# Words End of Day	Daily Novel Word Count	Cumulative Novel Word Count
PROJECT TITLE: **Daily Word Count Goal:** **Month:** **Date:**				
1	0		0	0
2	0		0	0

While it is good practice to set and track writing goals, it is important to include all your goals when planning the year ahead. The most important benefit of the tracking form is to encourage you to meet your goals and surpass them as you see the numbers add up.

Additional things that should have goals to complete and track:

- Editing, Research, Querying
- Book Cover Design
- Email Newsletter
- Social Media Posts
- Website Updates
- Ad Design, Placement & Schedule

Some of the items above are marketing related projects that take time in addition to your writing and book-related activities.

Other Important Tracking - Time, Talent & Treasure

Treating your writing as a business means you must acknowledge the time, talent, and treasure at your disposal. The first item, your "time," has a significant value because you invest time in writing your novels. Therefore, tracking reinforces that you are spending your time wisely and accomplishing the goal for each work in progress.

The second item, "talent," refers to your education, skills, and creativity. The focus on tracking time needs to include using your talent to develop, rework, edit, and polish your manuscripts. In addition, you may be the one writing all the marketing materials, placing the ads, and tracking the results.

Finally, the "treasure" item is the money you have available to invest in your writing business. There are the costs of editing, hiring a book coach, creative items for your manuscript like the design of book covers and formatting e-books, as well as hiring a virtual assistant. Then, you need to add marketing costs into your budgeting.

Implementing and tracking your writing goals ensures that you will have something to publish. Equally as important is to use the tools for tracking your time, talent, and treasure to ensure you are ready to publish and sell!

3 ACTION STEPS:

1. Take a moment and write down what your writing goals per day/week. It will give you an idea of what it takes to finish your manuscript. Add them into a document, whether a table in Word, an Excel worksheet, or a handwritten list for tracking. Include all marketing, social media, advertising, or website creative projects for your marketing plan that will take your time.

2. Next, list items that you may need to fund in your writing business like the editing, publishing, marketing, and other costs for a proposed budget.

3. Finally, write down the goal that will give you a feeling of writing success in terms of book sales. The goal helps you to be realistic about the sales you want to achieve and the importance of your marketing plan

Notes:

CHAPTER 3
The Author Brand to Support Your Writing Dream

What is a Personal Brand or Author Brand?

When a business creates a brand, it usually starts with a short statement or tagline that differentiates its products or services from the competition. For an author, the ability to help readers differentiate why they want to read your book(s) rather than another in the same genre, comes down to providing a quick statement or two about the uniqueness of your stories, writing style or voice.

Here are a few questions to help you get started in developing 1-2 sentences about your brand as the foundation of your author brand:

- What is your background (education, work, career, experience) that led you to write?

- What is the genre or subgenre you are writing?

- Why are your stories unique?

- Who is your target reader?

The key is to stand out in the crazy competitive marketplace, so your author brand can speak to what you do, who will enjoy your writing, and why they want to follow you. In essence, you want a clear answer to the question, "Why would I want to read your book?"

Here is an excellent example of an author brand, taken from the first two sentences of author, Hank Phillippi Ryan's website bio:

"HANK PHILLIPPI RYAN is the USA Today bestselling author of 14 psychological thrillers, winning the most prestigious awards in the genre: five Agathas, five Anthonys, and the coveted Mary Higgins Clark Award. She is also on-air investigative reporter for Boston's WHDH-TV, with 37 EMMYs and dozens more journalism honors." [7]

Obviously not all writers are Emmy-winning reporters like Ms. Ryan, yet if you write a really good nonfiction book and fiction novel, you still have career successes, education achievements, helpful skills, creativity, and more that can establish your author brand to be the foundation of your book marketing.

With a focused author brand statement, give the prospective reader insight into you, your work and why they will enjoy reading your book(s) in a couple sentences. Plus, your author brand includes using visual elements to attract readers:

- Logo — Pick a font for your name and tagline that represents your author brand image. It needs to be simple and easy to read. The key is to be consistent across all your marketing materials to make your name easy to recognize including on your website, in social media, email marketing, digital marketing, and printed materials.

- Color Palette — The colors on your website, in social media and email marketing should match your genre. Every genre has defining color palettes, for example the colors of red/black/gray for mysteries and thrillers, pastels for romances, and primary colors for cozy mysteries.

- Professional Photos — Always use a recent quality headshot of you on the website and in promotions. Also, use high quality graphics for your book cover, in social media, and in emails.

Author Brand Example

Patricia Sargeant (aka Olivia Matthews, Regina Hart) has published over 20 books, using pseudonyms for different genres. On her website, https://patriciasargeant.com/, the bio provides a link to watch her 30-second author brand video (https://youtu.be/ivASYzGogfs).[8] It's titled, A Story for Your Every Mood:

And, the description is, "National best-selling and award-winning author Patricia Sargeant – also writing as Olivia Matthews and Regina Hart – offers a story for readers' every mood, including cozy mystery, romantic suspense, small town romance, sports romance and contemporary romance." Note that her description is perfect as an elevator pitch to let someone new gain an understanding of what the author writes and why.

3 ACTION STEPS:

1. Create an author brand statement. Here is a simple jumpstart template:

   As an author of [genre], my readers will [be entertained with what type of story or feel what after reading my book], and my book [name of book or series] are easily found [where? online, bookstores, libraries] and in affordable formats [as eBook, paperback, audio] and more information can be found at my [website, Facebook, Instagram, other]. Try for 30-50 words only.

2. Distill it to a tagline. Focus on something that you want to pique the interest of someone new, particularly about what you promise from your book(s). Here is a tagline by author Rachael Herron for her podcast: "Irreverent, cheeky, business-focused and always honest, you're going to love this." Get it down to 10-15 words that you can recall easily.

3. Practice your author brand statement and tagline on friends, readers, and other writer buddies. The value of practicing both is to get used to delivering both with confidence. Once you have refined the wording to your satisfaction, you're ready to use them when meeting new people. Make sure to include both on your website and use the tagline for your email signature.

Notes:

CHAPTER 4
Building Your Author Success Plan

The Next Steps

Having run a marketing consulting firm, I believe a good marketing plan begins with branding as the foundation of your strategy, planning, and messaging. Then there are the three key things every writer should do to use their author brand and success plan to start building or enhancing their writing business:

Create an author success plan for your writing business.

1. Use the Author Promotion Quiz to focus attention on your strengths and any gaps that need attention.

2. Understand the basics of developing a marketing plan and supporting budget.

Let's delve into each one of these in more detail.

1. <u>Create an author success plan for your writing business.</u>

While many writers do not consider their efforts as a business, if you want to move from writing being a hobby to making money at your craft, you need to think like a business owner. And most business owners do better when there is a plan with a budget. While this handbook is focused on marketing, to be effective, you need a business plan to align those marketing activities to support making money by selling books.

> **The secret of getting ahead is getting started. The secret of getting started is breaking your complex overwhelming tasks into small manageable tasks, and starting on the first one.**
>
> **Mark Twain[9]**

Items for Your Plan

Focusing on the list below of those items to consider for your plan. Use the questions to help you start developing a simple and manageable plan for your writing biz:

1. **Executive Summary** – In brief, document what you intend to accomplish in the next 1-3 years with your writing business. Do your goals include wanting to be traditionally published, independently published, or hybrid? Are you looking to be a best-selling author, award-winning, and/or to have your book(s) optioned for movie or TV?

2. **Writing Business Goals** – Detail what you want to accomplish in the next 3 years. What are 3 goals to consider for this year? How many book(s) or series do you want to write? What would be the projected sales and income in the next one, two and three years?

3. **Personal Life Goals** – Because writing takes time, focus and talent, the process can overtake a lot of your life. What are three goals you want to achieve that require time or resources that take away from your writing business?

4. **Products to Sell** – Determine the books/series you will produce and in what genres. Who are your target readers for each? What is the anticipated schedule you will need to complete and publish each?

5. **Comparable Analysis** – Research to find comparable titles. or "comp titles." is important to know how your book(s) are unique yet similar to others that readers already enjoy. Do you know which authors in your genre have similar book(s)? For newer authors, who are the mid-range, not best-selling authors, who are most like read by your target readers? What framework of comp titles can you cite so readers know what to expect from your book(s)?

6. **Marketing/Promotion** – When you know your goals, products, and competition the next step is to create marketing to attract and build a reader base for your book sales. For example, the three marketing strategies that are manageable and affordable for writers are email marketing, social media marketing, and digital advertising. Have you developed an email list? Do you have a website with email sign-up? What social media platforms are you currently using; Facebook, Instagram, TikTok/BookTok, Twitter? Are you interested in running ads on social media or on Amazon?

7. **Operations** – The key is to focus on your writing to create wonderful books, so freeing up your time is critical. To run the business side of your writing, it is important to define what expertise or assistance you require. Do you need help with administrative tasks, editing, book coaching, design for your cover and book layout, and marketing pieces? Can you hire a virtual assistant, or do you need to take some online courses to help become proficient at ad campaigns?

8. **Budget** – List the costs that will enable you to bring your writing to the market. Then, create a few revenue scenarios to cover the budgeted costs as well as make your writing business a profit. Do you need that virtual assistant, a graphic designer for book covers, or professional editing help? Do you need to take an online course or master class? What does your website hosting, web developer, and domain cost per year? Is there an amount you are comfortable with for digital advertising?

9. **Action Items** – List your three author business goals and three personal goals. For each, what are three initial actions you can take to start? How can you focus your attention on working towards them? What are achievable due dates for each action?

10. **Evaluation of the Plan** – As the final item in your business planning, it is key to review each step to see if you are getting good results. How will you measure your goals? What will you monitor to determine the success of the plan starting with book sales and then responses to ads, website visits, email subscriptions, email open rates?

Creating a Writing Business Plan

Questions to help you start developing a simple business plan for your writing biz:

- **Executive Summary** – In brief, document what you intend to accomplish in the next 1-3 years with your writing business.

  o Do you want to be traditionally published, self-published, or hybrid?

  o Are you looking to be a best-selling author, award-winning, and/or optioned for movie or TV?

- **Writing Business Goals** – Detail what you want to accomplish in the next 3 years.

  o What are 3 goals to consider for this year?

  o How many book(s) or series do you want to write?

  o What would be the projected sales and income in the next one, two and three years?

- **Personal Life Goals** – Because writing takes time, focus and talent, the process overtakes a lot of your life.

  o What are three goals you want to achieve that you may need time or resources for that may impact your writing business?

- **Products to Sell** – Determine the books/series you will produce and in what genres.

  o Who are your target readers for each?

  o What is the anticipated schedule you will need to complete and publish each?

- **Competitive Analysis** – Research is important to know how your book(s) are unique yet similar to others that readers already enjoy.

  o Do you know which authors are in your genre that have similar book(s)?

  o For newer authors, who are the mid-range, not best-selling authors, who are most like read by your target readers?

  o What framework of comparable titles can you offer for readers to know what to expect from your book(s)?

- **Marketing/Promotion** – When you know your goals, products, and competition the next step is to create the marketing elements to attract and build a reader base for book sales. There are three major strategies that are manageable for writers. These are email marketing, social media marketing, and digital advertising.

    o Have you developed an email list?

    o Do you have a website with an email sign-up?

    o What social media platforms are you currently using; Facebook, Instagram, TikTok/BookTok, Twitter?

    o Are you interested in running ads in social media or on Amazon?

- **Operations** – Key is to focus on your writing, so freeing up your time is critical. To run the business side of your writing, it is key to define who you can afford to hire.

    o Do you need help with admin tasks, editing, book coaching, design for cover and book layout, and marketing elements?

    o Can you hire a virtual assistant or need to take some online courses to help become proficient at ad campaigns?

- **Budget** – List the costs that will enable you to bring your writing to market. Then, create a few revenue scenarios to afford the budgeted costs as well as make your writing business a profit.

    o Do you need that virtual assistant, graphic designer for book covers, or editing help?

    o Do you need to take an online course or master class?

    o What does your website hosting, web developer, and domain cost per year?

    o Is there an amount you are comfortable with for digital advertising?

- **Action Steps** – List your three writing business goals and three personal goals.

    o For each goal, what are three initial steps you can take to get started?

    o How can you focus your attention on working towards them?

    o What are achievable due dates for each step?

- **Evaluation of the Plan** – As the final item in your business planning, it is key to review each step and each campaign to see if you are getting good results.

    o How will you measure your goals?

    o What speaks to you to monitor the success of the plan?

Break Down Goals into Critical Steps

Once you have sketched out the elements above for your overall plan, you will break them down into smaller steps. These are the critical ones that make it easier to achieve momentum and results for your plan. Also, the steps need to be small or simple enough to encourage you to keep moving forward. If the goals and actions you need to take are too big, you may be overwhelmed and not know where to start.

To make it easy for you to do your tracking, below is an idea of a simple way to help organize those critical steps. This also works for your marketing plan items. In both instances, the key is to make sure you track results.

You can easily duplicate this tracking form to keep moving forward with critical steps. It can be done as a table in a Word or Excel document, or by hand in a notebook.

Goal 1:				
Action Item	**Responsible Person**	**Milestone Date**	**How Measured?**	**Results**
1.				
2.				
3.				

Goal 2:				
Action Item	**Responsible Person**	**Milestone Date**	**How Measured?**	**Results**
1.				
2.				
3.				

Use the Author Promotion Quiz to focus attention on your strengths and any gaps that need attention.

For both aspiring and published authors, a marketing plan is critical to ensure ongoing promotion and encourage sales. Aspiring authors, those who have not yet been published, may think the promotion quiz is putting the cart before the horse. A traditionally published author may assume the publisher will take care of the marketing. Yet in both cases, it is important to have the author brand and marketing platform ready. In essence, both aspiring and published authors need to take the same initial steps to magnify marketing results when publishing a nonfiction book or fiction novel.

With 3 million titles uploaded to Amazon every year and traditional publishers seeking writers with an established author platform, every author needs to understand and embrace the importance of promoting their "product(s)." Prime the pump by building your marketing machine to be ready for a book launch.

To kickstart a review of your marketing plan, take the Author Self-Promotion Quiz. The quiz is a great way to assess your current marketing or promotion strengths and uncover gaps. It includes the check and balance of marketing tools and activities everyone should be using for launches and to attract recurring sales.

Another benefit of this exercise is to get an idea of what your goals should be in the new marketing plan. Your goals should be the first focus of your plan to make sure every step you take, all the time used, and every dollar you spend – in essence, your time, talent and treasure – is directed to achieving those goals.

Author Self Promotion Quiz

Take this test to see how effective you are at promoting yourself and your writing!	Yes/No
1.	In 30 seconds, can you clearly state your author brand, the genre(s) you write, the series, and what you love about writing?	
2.	Do you have a website that includes your author brand and information on what you are writing or books available?	
3.	In the last few months, have you googled to see what is out on the Internet about you and updated any membership or author pages?	
4.	Do you have a Success Network of friends, other authors, publishing contacts that is up to date?	

5.	Are you involved in volunteer activities to expand your Success Network including organizations like Sisters in Crime and other professional organizations?	
6.	Have you developed an email list of friends, family, acquaintances and readers to keep in contact with an e-newsletter?	
7.	Do you have an email capture on your website that offers an onboarding/welcome set of emails?	
8.	Have you sent a personal note, an email or made a phone call to someone in your Success Network in the past month just to keep in touch and share where your book projects have gotten to so far?	
9.	In the last six months, have you given a presentation or served on a panel on a topic that relates to your writing or something that you are passionate about?	
10.	Do you have a current headshot and book cover(s) in a JPG format ready to send by email?	

Understand the basics of developing a marketing plan and supporting budget.

With your annual goals identified and answers from the Authors Promotion Quiz, you will see what needs to be addressed. You will also be able to zero in on the most essential marketing and promotion items.

As a quick foundation, meet the 4 Ps of Marketing to get you organized: Product, Price, Place, and Promotion. In studying marketing, students are taught a very simple formula – that you have the "right" Product available at the "right" Price at a convenient Place by attracting to target readers with the "right" Promotion. The overall objective is to influence the behavior of potential readers through effective communication. The answers to the following questions can help create the marketing plan.

Product – Your Book

Because your books are products, the key is to let prospective readers know what to expect from your author brand and the reading experience of your book(s).

- What is your genre? Nonfiction: business, personal development, religious? Fiction: mystery, romance, fantasy, historical?

- What is your author brand elevator pitch or tagline?

- What is the storyline in your book? Will the reader be taken on a journey, be informed or have other experience?

- Who is your book's target audience? Age group – adult, young adult, middle grade, children?

- How is your book different from what others offer? Is there a special spin? How is it similar to other books or series that have been successful sellers?

Pricing of Your Book

There are pricing strategies to consider with books as well as for a series. These often depend on whether traditionally or independently published. Or you may be a hybrid author with a mix of books/series one is with a traditional publisher, and another is indie-published such as on Amazon.

- What is the price range of your book according to the genre you write for print versions and e-books?

- What is the price range of your target reader? Higher or lower than others in your genre?

- What price is too high for your readers? What price is too low?

- What price best fits your target reader?

Place to Distribute Your Book

Distribution of your book(s) is through channels including retail and online options. Your choice of setting up those channels relies on several factors. First, if traditionally published, your publisher will be responsible for getting your book(s) into bookstores, libraries, and other retailers. Second, if you choose to independently publish, the ways you offer your book for sale rely on you. Third, all authors are facing tremendous competition, so knowing where to offer your books for sale is important to make it easy for target readers to purchase them.

Here are three key questions to make sure you are reviewing all the different options.

- Where does your target reader shop? Online, at large chain stores, or at smaller independent bookstores?

- Where will your book(s) be available for sale? Are there other retail options to consider?

- What distribution channel(s) should be used when making special offers to encourage purchases? Email, retail or online to make it easy for your target readers?

Promote Your Book

The objective of promotion is to inform, persuade, and remind potential readers/fans about your book or series. Promotion is often multi-layered to pique the interest of target readers, encourage them to engage with your work and get them ready to buy your books.

- What is the best time to reach your target reader?

- What marketing channels are most effective for your target reader?

- What advertising approaches are most persuasive to your target reader?

Creating Your Answers into a Marketing Plan

To start, here are two worksheets that briefly describe a mini marketing plan and provide a list of items for a budget. While we will go into more dept in the next chapter, it is important to understand how using simple marketing basics can help increase your confidence and bring in more sales. Included in the mini plan are the Five Components of Your Marketing Plan which are:

- Marketing Goals

- Promotion to Support Goals

- Marketing Calendar

- Budget

- Evaluation of Results

Working with the checklist, developing a plan will enable you to be more organized in your approach to growing book sales. For aspiring writers, setting up the plan prior to finishing a manuscript gives you the opportunity to get your ducks in a row. For published authors, even if by a traditional publisher, using a marketing plan supports and boosts the success of your book.

Another key aspect of being an organized writer/author is that having an author brand supported by a marketing plan makes you more valuable. In today's competitive marketplace, if publishers see that you have already prepared your marketing, it could help you to get a contract. Then, when your marketing helps sales, it could ensure they will publish your next book in a series or another project by you.

For an indie-published author, being ready with your author brand supported with a marketing plan gives you a leg up on launching your book. Plus, having books sales will encourage you to keep writing. encourage you to keep writing. For an indie-published author, being ready with your author brand supported with a marketing plan gives you a leg up on launching your book. Plus, having books sales will encourage you to keep writing.

Budget to Support Your Marketing Plan

Because there are items that will need funding, a brief way to organize your budget is to consider grouping them into key areas such as:

- Author Brand

- Promotions

- Business Services

The items that you should consider include everything from business cards to digital ads to hiring a virtual assistant. A quick review of the list on the worksheet will help you recognize items you may need to pay for versus others you can handle on your own.

Five Components of Your Marketing Plan

1. Marketing Goals

2. Promotions to Support Goals

3. Budget

4. Marketing Calendar

5. Evaluation of Results

   1. **Marketing Goals (Set 3 to attract more readers, sell more books)**

      Questions to assess where your marketing currently stands and create new goals:

      ❑ What are your goals for your book business?

      ❑ Where are you now?

      ❑ What should your next steps be?

      ❑ What obstacles are in your way?

      ❑ Have you done practical exercises to move forward?

   2. **Promotions to Support Goals**

      ❑ Email campaigns

      ❑ Digital Ad campaigns

      ❑ Social Media campaigns

      ❑ Website promotions and updates

❑ Book Fairs, Launches, and Conferences

❑ Other

3. **Marketing Calendar (Annual list of promotion and activities for consistency)**

❑ Timing – Recommend monthly

❑ Medium – Include e-marketing, digital ads, social media

❑ Promotion – Provide the theme for each campaign

❑ Target – detail the reader profile

4. **Budget (Keep it simple)**

❑ Author Brand Items

❑ Promotions

❑ Business Services

5. **Evaluation of Results**

❑ How to determine the Recovery of Marketing Costs

❑ Calculating Return on Investment (ROI) for Marketing

Marketing Budget	Annual Budgeted Amount	YTD Expenditure
Author Brand		
Graphics - Professional Assistance	$0.00	$0.00
Business Cards & Giveaways	$0.00	$0.00
Special Gifts, Misc. Specialty Items	$0.00	$0.00
Website - Development	$0.00	$0.00
Website - Ongoing Updates	$0.00	$0.00
Display Board for Special Events	$0.00	$0.00
Other	$0.00	$0.00
Annual Budgeted Amount	$0.00	$0.00

Amount under or over budget		$0.00
Promotions		
Ad Campaign(s)	$0.00	$0.00
Email Campaign(s)	$0.00	$0.00
Social Media Campaign(s)	$0.00	$0.00
Other	$0.00	$0.00
Annual Budgeted Amount	$0.00	$0.00
Amount under or over budget		$0.00
Business Services		
Memberships (Writing & Business)	$0.00	$0.00
Programs/Webinars/Education Seminars	$0.00	$0.00
Part-time Intern/Assistant	$0.00	$0.00
Other Professional Services	$0.00	$0.00
Annual Budgeted Amount and Total to Date	$0.00	$0.00
Amount under or over budget		$0.00
Total Budgeted for Marketing	$0.00	
Total Expended YTD		$0.00
Amount under or over budget		$0.00

3 ACTION STEPS:

1. Review the Writing Business Plan Checklist. As you can work through the sections, it will help you to better understand how to create a writing business.

2. Set 3 goals to achieve within the year. The process of setting goals is a critical step. It's important to be honest with yourself on the effort you want to make in your writing business. With goals, you can better focus on the best ways to use your time, talent, and treasure.

3. Work through the Mini Marketing Plan Checklist. Use ideas and questions to guide you. Decide what you feel comfortable doing as you tackle marketing to increase book sales. And the budget worksheet is the means to recognize the funds it will take because books will not sell themselves!

Notes:

CHAPTER 5
Getting Started on Your Marketing Plan

Key Elements for Your Marketing

Your time is often focused on writing great stories rather than fussing with business stuff like marketing. Yet, for your book to be a success, you need to attract readers.

The old adage in marketing is this: If you think everyone is your customer, *then no one is.*

To increase sales, you must know your target reader. Once you have a profile in mind, you can structure your promotions, e-newsletters, digital ads, and social media to reach people who match it. Understanding your target reader makes it easier to write the copy, pick the digital ad audience reach, and social media content.

> **Everyone is not your customer. Seth Godin**[10]

Let's explore each to make it easier to jumpstart marketing projects.

Focus on Your Target Reader

One misconception that often occurs that often happens when an author is ready to present her/his story to the world is that everyone will want to read it. While that's a great wish, there has never been a book that appealed to all readers. So, if the description of your target reader is too broad it means missing out on building a real reader/fan base.

Many marketing gurus recommend starting with the demographics and psychographics that best identify your "tribe" – the initial group who build a base. The key is to develop a narrow profile of your target reader to attract someone who will truly enjoy your book. Once you do, it is easier to create marketing copy that attracts those readers who will buy, share reviews, and tell others about your book.

The Target Reader Profile

Tightening up your idea about who you're writing for makes it easier to create your marketing and find more of the right readers. Sometimes authors have told me that everyone will enjoy their book or series. These authors are hesitant to narrow the scope because they believe a focused target reader profile will limit their sales. Unfortunately, too wide a target and the marketing and promotion messaging will be too broad and miss passionate readers. When you create the messaging to engage with those readers who can become your tribe, your marketing will turn into books sales.

To start, sometimes it helps to make up a name for your "star" reader. Crafting a persona like "Amanda," "Delia," or "James" helps you talk to her/him when writing your marketing copy for e-news, digital ads, podcasts, and videos. You can use the questions below to guide you in researching the person who will most likely enjoy and buy your book(s).

1. Make a list of demographics:

    ❑ How old is she/he?

    ❑ Where does she/he live?

    ❑ What does she/he do for a living?

    ❑ What about education level?

    ❑ Is she/he married?

    ❑ Does she/he have kids?

    ❑ What social media does she/he use?

    ❑ What kind of hobbies?

2. Make a list of psychographics:

    ❑ What is her/his emotional connection with reading?

    ❑ Does she/he value time to read or spent with family?

    ❑ Does she/he focus on complicated situations or like simple reads?

    ❑ Besides your genre, does she/he read other ones?

    ❑ Is she/he favoring a healthy lifestyle or fulfillment in her career?

    ❑ Is she/he affiliated with any groups or organizations that are political, religious or gender specific?

3. Next, ask yourself how this information represents your target reader.

    ❑ How is your book or series written for someone like her/him?

    ❑ When you write, will it delight that person?

    ❑ Would she/he like it as much as you enjoyed writing it?

    ❑ What groups are you already a part of?

    ❑ Does your target reader hang out in the same social media, too?

4. Another quick exercise for refining your target reader description:

❑ What key words do other authors use to write books similar to yours to attract readers on Amazon?

❑ Who is leaving positive reviews? Note their gender. Guess their ages.

❑ What profile is most common for your genre?

❑ Have you reviewed books similar to yours that are suggested as "Frequently bought together" and "Explore Similar Books" that Amazon offers at the bottom of the page? Review what the descriptions are for attracting readers to promote another purchase.

Marketing Outreach & Promotion Ideas

With a target reader profile, it is easier to put together marketing outreach ideas. Take a research trip to look at the social media sites and/or groups you belong to – both online and in person. These are the starting places to find more opportunities for your marketing and ads.

Below is a checklist to help choose your marketing efforts to support your writing business and book sales. With limited time, it is important for you to be able to focus on marketing with ease. For example, e-mail is a direct link with readers, so building the email list with an e-newsletter will require your time. If you determine that your target reader is likely on Instagram, become proficient with that app over other social media apps. And, if you want to draw potential readers to buy more in a series or from a backlist, using your website means keeping it up to date and filled with good content.

The Quick-Start Checklist

Most writers recognize the need for marketing, but many do not have the background or experience to know what is best to do or where to start. With a background in marketing, it was easy to put together a helpful checklist for my author friends.

Here is the organizing tool that I created to help any author get started:

☐ Author Brand

☐ Target Reader Outline

☐ Tagline and Description

☐ Logo including Font(s)

☐ Color Palette

☐ Business Card

☐ E-signature

- [ ] Website

  - [ ] Domain and Website Hosting

  - [ ] About Us/Blog/Contact Us/Social Media Links

  - [ ] Email sign-up form

  - [ ] Schedule updates – Once per month for blog

- [ ] Email List Builder

  - [ ] Email Sign -Up Form – Have a simple subscription form on your home page to capture someone's email address for your email newsletter.

  - [ ] Offer for a Freebie – Called a "reader magnet," offer a short story, first chapter or prequel novella if someone signs up with their email address.

  - [ ] Mail Chimp/BookFunnel/ClickFunnel – Using a service helps you design, send, and track results of your emails as well as maintain the database of emails.

  - [ ] Create a Schedule – To be consistent, set up either once per week or month an email to be sent to keep in touch with your subscribers.

- [ ] Social Media

  - [ ] Facebook

  - [ ] Instagram

  - [ ] Twitter

  - [ ] YouTube

  - [ ] BookTok/TikTok

  - [ ] Schedule – minimum once per week and more as you are able to create posts

- [ ] Pre-Order & Advance Reader Team

  - [ ] Goodreads/Book Bub/BookFunnel – Offer ads and services.

  - [ ] Kirkus Reviews – For launch day highlight good reviews.

  - [ ] Social media – Ask beta and advanced copy readers to post reviews.

  - [ ] Book Bloggers & Podcasters – Gain publicity with their audiences.

  - [ ] Facebook groups – Create one and use it as a street team effort.

  - [ ] Author Marketing Groups – Literature & Latte, Career Authors and others offer opportunities to get in front of new audiences.

  - [ ] Library Outreach – Many offer sections for local authors.

☐ Award Programs – If you enter competitions in your genre, you may be award-nominated or award-winning to add into your marketing materials.

Content & Schedule

The next step is to calendar your marketing for the year including when you want to run promotions or ad campaigns, send e-newsletters, and do posts on social media. It is helpful to add content ideas and put due dates on the calendar. It helps focus your time and avoid wasting precious hours every week trying to throw something together for social media or e-newsletters.

Below is an example of an easy worksheet that I adapted for book marketing that includes scheduling and tracking dates for marketing projects every month. The key is to use columns to detail the project or goal, the medium, the working title or theme of the content, and a place to note if it was accomplished. The final item would be a "Notes" column to document changes you needed to make or ideas that came up when creating various content pieces.

Book Marketing Content & Schedule

Month:

Date	Project Book, Series, Short Story, Launch, Other	Medium Email, Website, Blog, Social Media, Events, etc.	Working Title	Done Y/N	Notes

The most important aspect of tracking is to document your progress and make tactical changes as needed. Without a system, you are relegated to last-minute efforts that are not able to really support your marketing goals.

3 ACTION STEPS:

1. **Define your target reader:** Name, description, and likely social media she/he uses.

2. **What do I need to learn** to be proficient in email marketing, social media and digital ads that will reach my target reader?

3. **Where in the Quick-Start Checklist** do I need more help, skill, or information to be more proficient?

Notes:

CHAPTER 6
Your Marketing Tool Chest

Strategy to Get Readers Excited to Buy

The purpose of your marketing plan is to create a strategy that supports the goals you set for your book sales each year and helps you accomplish them. By using the marketing tools discussed in these chapters, you can attract the attention of readers and move them to buy your books. As a consumer, you are constantly bombarded with ads and content from companies trying to sell you a product or a service. These companies are attempting to engage with their target consumers using email, ads, social media, and other content that creates a compelling positive emotional reaction.

Your marketing as a writer needs to make the target reader aware of your book(s) and excited to purchase them. In the congested, competitive marketplace today on Amazon or in a bookstore, your efforts need to focus on getting the target reader ready to buy your book. In essence, you need to be proactive in finding ways to connect with them and be visible to promote book sales.

Many successful authors have embraced this and crafted special relationships with their fans/readers. A good example of a professional who has a great marketing machine is James Patterson. No surprise, he was an advertising executive prior to his writing career. He had a background that perfectly served him for building book sales. Writers from professional careers in education, government, law, accounting, medicine, and other professions did not gain the same kind of marketing knowledge to help sell their stories.

Consider the list of marketing tools on the following pages to determine the ones you feel most comfortable using.

The Items in Your Tool Chest

To get target readers excited to buy your book or follow you as an author, the starting point to support your marketing plan is to utilize the promotional tools effectively. As you prepare your plan, gather ideas, and determine a budget, it is helpful to look over the many marketing and promotional tools at your disposal. Some of the tools may require more training or hiring an expert, while other tools are easy to use with little cost.

In the Author Self Promotion Quiz in Chapter 4, you may find elements to update, add or change for your promotion. Let's explore those "tools" from the quiz to build your marketing:

1. **Elevator pitch** – The idea of an "elevator pitch" relates to what you can tell someone in the short period of an elevator ride, about 30 seconds. It's the idea to offer a quick insight into you as an author or your current project. There are two versions that are good to have ready. The first is having your author brand pitch for prospective readers about the genre(s) you write, your experience as an author, and what you love about writing. The second version is for an agent, editor, or publisher, about the current book or series you're writing. Be ready for those opportunities and avoid stumbling around when you have the opportunity to talk about you or your book. *Tip: These should each be about 50-75 words.*

2. **Current headshot and book cover(s)** – Make sure you have quality photo files in PNG and JPG formats ready to send by email or post in social media. *Tip: Do not use a headshot on the website or book cover that is over 10 years old because readers/fans want to identify with you. If they see a much younger you on the "About" page, then watch a video where you have aged significantly, it causes a disconnect.*

3. **Website** – Key is to have a distinctive color palette, your author brand tagline, and information on what you are writing or books available. Think of it as your office online for your writing business. *Tip: It is critical to ensure people know they can count on checking your website for book launches, new material, and events to attend.*

4. **Email List** – Building a list of subscribers is important especially for your devoted fans, friends and family who want to know what's happening in your writing business. While it does take time to develop, the value of having a good email list is being able to regularly reach a fan base to enhance book launches and sales. *Tip: A starter is to send an email asking friends, family, acquaintances, and readers to join your e-newsletter list.*

5. **Subscriber Love** – To stay in contact with prospects and readers, you need an email sign-up form on your website. Especially when someone visits your website, offer a form that is easy for the visitor to sign up with their email address. There are all kinds of widgets for capturing email addresses that can be added to your website home page. Some authors will offer a freebie if the person signs up. For example, these freebies are called "lead magnets" to attract leads for you to email about your book(s). *Tip: It is best to set up a welcome email to acknowledge the sign-up, as well as thank and engage with the new subscriber.*

6. **Author Page** – If self-published, make the most of your Amazon author page as well as other places your author story/bio appears. *Tip: Google your name to see what photos, news, videos, books and more come up on the Internet tied to your name that may require updating or removing.*

7. **Success Network** – In marketing yourself and your writing biz, develop a network that may be slightly different from your email list. This is a group of friends, other authors, publishing contacts, and others who can help through learning your craft, publishing, and promoting your

book(s). ***Tip: Take the time to decide who in your network can be of value in promoting you and your books to their own networks.***

8. **Professional Organizations** – For expanding your Success Network, a great place to start is joining organizations like Sisters in Crime, Romance Writers of America, Mystery Writers of America, and other professional organizations as well as local chapters of writers. ***Tip: Be active by offering to volunteer. You will meet more of the members and other volunteers and expand your Success Network.***

9. **Contact List** – The idea of having a Success Network or at least an email list of key contacts helps every author as a resource for gaining more visibility and reader awareness. And it also requires you to send a personal note, an email or make a phone call to someone on the list every month just to keep in touch and share about your book projects. ***Tip: Keep a running list of those you contact including the date, the subject and the response.***

10. **Presentations** – Attending conferences is a good way to meet others in the writing business as well as fans. It's even more powerful to be a presenter or panelist at the conference. In addition, there are organization meetings, local workshops, and online gatherings that are interested in new guest speakers and new topics. Create a presentation you can offer to event coordinators. Or propose to serve on a panel for a topic that relates to your writing or something that you are passionate about. ***Tip: In Chapter 8, you will find a step-by-step process on being prepared for public speaking. Do consider choosing two or three topics that you would like to speak about or be willing to conduct training on and be ready when an opportunity arises.***

More on Marketing Content & Promotion Methods

As you begin to feel more confident or recognize the action you want to take to promote your writing biz, let's dive into these important tools:

- **The Author Story**
- **A Professional Website – Your Office**
- **The Email List**
- **Digital Ads**
- **Social Media**

The Author Story

Stories light up the imagination. Use storytelling about you as an author and your writing projects to engage prospective readers. A story helps to give your readers the idea of what they will discover from your book(s). A starter is to define the difference that your book makes in the life of your reader.

Here are three steps:

1. **Use your author brand tagline, brand description, and pitch to engage with your readers.** Remember that your tagline needs to be short and punchy. It must pique the interest of your target or prospective reader. You want her/him to seek more about your writing business and follow your social media. The author brand description should be the longer story to let them know about your writing journey. And the pitch is meant to quickly interest the target reader in your book(s).

2. **Focus on developing a story of how your book(s) will entertain and engage prospective readers.** With a longer story, you can carve it into snippets to have more options for your marketing content. Another great way to illustrate your author story is to use a review from a beta reader. A review is from a real person as a quick story that illustrates what they enjoyed about your book.

3. **Create ways to incorporate your author brand story and pitch in marketing content.** To achieve your goals as well as build the interest from target readers, use your story in various ways within social media posts, digital ads, and email marketing. You know when the messaging is hitting the mark when you have more clicks and people buying your book(s).

A Professional Website - Your Office

As your writing business office, having an author website provides you with a space where readers and fans can learn more about you and your book(s). It is also meant to be a place apart from any of your other professional, career or job-related websites. Using social media is helpful in engaging with target readers, but it is constantly updating. With an "office" online, it showcases your writing business and gives an element of legitimacy. Both traditionally and independently published authors utilize websites to offer their bio, current book(s), contact information, email sign-up form, a backlist of books, speaking events, links to purchase, and more.

If you're an aspiring author, create your website as soon as possible. It will help build your writing business and encourage a fan base before you launch your first book. If you are a published author, consider auditing your current website. Review every part of your website and update anything that is not current. Examine how it compares to other author websites in your genre.

Here are three quick tips about your website for aspiring and published authors:

1. **Refresh your site often.** My recommendation is to check things monthly. From specials, promotional offers, or freebies, the key is to change these often on the home page. With interesting information or graphics, when a visitor comes back to the site, it's more interesting or engaging. Keep the look "fresh" by routinely making changes considering these questions:

   - Is it serving your career goals well?

- Is it easy for readers to navigate?

- Does it help them connect with you and your writing?

- Do you respond in a timely manner?

- Does your website generate interest and make a reader want to explore more of it?

2. **Provide multiple ways for a visitor to communicate with you.** First, consider a simple fill-in "contact me" form rather than providing your email address. The form should be short to capture basic information and a message. Then, be sure to respond to the visitor in a timely manner, within a business day or sooner.

Next, offer an email sign-up form or pop-up to subscribe to your e-newsletter and announcements. With the email capture form, include a privacy policy statement that you won't use their email address for any other purpose or sell it to advertisers.

3. **Add social media accounts to your website.** The website is where interested readers go to find out more about you and your books, so having web links to your social media gives them another way to engage. Only link social media icons to those accounts you keep updated on a regular basis. The reason for using only active social media accounts is if you have not uploaded a post, video, or photo in the last month to a platform, your readers/fans will lose interest.

The Email List

As a direct connection to family, friends, and readers, it is important to have an active email list that you send engaging messages to consistently. If the people on your list have signed up and did not unsubscribe, emails from you, as a favorite author, get different attention than social media. It is more personal of a touch.

Think of email messages and e-newsletters as a key part of your book marketing foundation to support book launches, sell more of your backlist, and create a core of target readers for new projects. From offering insights into your book(s), to promoting a new book, or selling your backlist of prior published books, email marketing is a great, low-cost outreach. And, if your content is interesting and engaging, you can remind readers to invite others to sign up for your list.

While it is key to send interesting emails, the concept is to attract, build and maintain your list. Therefore, to initially capture more email addresses, as mentioned before, have a sign-up form that pops up on your website. You can encourage website visitors to provide their email addresses to receive your email updates and e-newsletters. One effective way to attract someone to fill out the email form is to use a giveaway. Here are some easy steps:

- Create a PDF of something that you can use as a giveaway such as a short story, a first chapter, or a character study.

- With each sign-up, send a "thank you" email with your free reader magnet.

- Write a follow-up email to touch base after a week or two to ask the receiver about it and if they have questions for you about your book(s).

- Develop an ongoing sequence of emails for the year to be consistent in being in front of your subscribers. Commit to a monthly e-newsletter, a three-part serialized short story or chapters of a novella that can go out weekly or every other week.

- Consider holding a giveaway to win one of your books or to partner with another author to share email lists. Ask your email subscribers to invite new people to join your list and get an extra chance to win. And promote the giveaway on your website to generate interest in subscribing to your list.

Another wonderful way authors have used email lists is to do e-newsletter swaps with other authors to expand your reach. To get started, you can offer to swap email lists with another writer in your genre. It's as simple as giving your e-newsletter to another author who sends it with a mention of you being an author the reader might like. Then, you send out the other author's e-newsletter to your list with the same type of mention. There is great value in uncovering more interested target readers without any dollar cost.

A quick story, a thriller writer friend had been traditionally published for years but the royalties were not big enough to put her kids through college. She had heard that romance was a huge market for Amazon e-books. She told me at dinner one night that she used a pen name for romance books to avoid any issues with her publisher. She also adopted the idea to build a reader fan base by swapping email lists. She thought it would work to jumpstart her debut as a romance writer and generate more book sales. It did. And in a little less than a year later, she had made more on her romance books with Amazon in one month than she was paid in the entire year of royalty checks for her thrillers.

Social Media

There are two huge benefits to using social media to promote your book(s). First, interaction is key with most people checking and engaging with their favorite apps every day. Second, you can use one piece of content with slight changes across all the platforms.

A Note about Hashtags

Consider using hashtags for your social media posts. You have likely seen them in posts, and they can be helpful in attracting new eyes to your social media. The description from Wikipedia[11] is: "A hashtag is a metadata tag that is prefaced by the hash symbol, #. On social media, hashtags are used on microblogging and photo-sharing services such as Twitter or Tumblr as a form of user-generated tagging that enables cross-referencing of content by topic or theme."

If you want to find a good hashtag to add to your posts, use website **best-hashtags.com**[12]. When I asked for the best book related hashtags, here were a few:

#bookreviews

#bookstagram

#bookreview,

#booktok

You likely have accounts on the most popular social media platforms that you enjoy the most. If you already are posting or uploading content, it will be a natural extension to promote your book(s). It is important to consider creating an author profile account on your favorite platforms which gives you a better focus on your writing business, not mixed in with your personal accounts.

Here is a list of the most popular social media apps:

- Instagram
- Facebook
- Threads
- YouTube
- Twitter
- BookTok/TikTok
- Pinterest
- LinkedIn

When deciding on the social media platforms you intend to use for your writing business, consider two things, where your target readers engage and your time. The first factor is to uncover what social media your target readers can find engaging. If you are not sure, research by checking those where authors of a similar book or series are posting. Consider searching through their followers to see if they fit your target reader profile.

The second factor is to determine how much time you are willing to invest in creating content, posting, and responding. Most authors choose one or two apps because of how much time multiple social media platforms can take away from writing and other marketing touches that build sales.

Public Relations and Publicity

Public relations and publicity are often thought to be the same in marketing. From Wikipedia, "Public relations (PR) is the practice of managing and disseminating information from an individual or an organization to the public in order to influence their perception. Public relations and publicity differ in that PR is controlled internally, whereas publicity is not controlled and contributed by external parties." The reason to understand the difference is that public relations is a practice by a professional handler that works to contact media and try to manage media mentions to sell books. Publicity is the sending out press releases and contacting media to hopefully have something good published about your book(s) but not able to manage media contacts or ensure good results.

In your marketing plan, public relations can be key in building and maintaining a positive public image for your author brand. It includes media relations, online and social media communications, and managing special events. For traditionally published authors, many publishers do media releases, set up special events, and contact media outlets for your launch. Yet, to build ongoing sales, you will need to support these efforts with additional public relations by paying for a public relations professional to help you or tackling them yourself.

For independently published authors, it does fall to you to create media releases, develop events, and manage online communications. You can hire a public relations professional if you have the funds to help you jumpstart more book sales. Ongoing public relations efforts will help keep your book(s) in the media to help build sales.

Here are some additional ideas to include in your marketing plan to gain exposure:

- **Book Launches** – As an event, you can decide to do it online via Zoom, or at a venue like an independent bookstore, library, or a church. Press can be invited as well as target readers, and friends. Most importantly, you can offer a special reading, sell books, and conduct an author interview.

- **Local Newspapers** – In smaller communities and suburbs, there are still newspapers that are being delivered in mailboxes. You can send a media release to announce your book launch with your headshot and book cover graphic files. It gives the newspaper material to highlight a resident and it doesn't cost you anything.

- **Podcasters & Bloggers** – Look for those podcasts that your target reader may be listening to or blogs that match your target reader. Send the blogger or podcast host an offer to talk about your new book or series, highlighting something unique that their listeners/readers would be interested in.

- **Book Store Readings** – Make a list of local independent bookstores that are in your community or where you could afford to travel to visit. Offer to do a special reading and book signing for your book launch or any time they have a spot available.

A writer friend decided to publish her first book at the heralded age of 84. Part of her novel had to do with human trafficking, and she decided to donate a portion of her book sales to a non-profit organization that helps victims. Because her church was supporting the organization, she decided to hold the book launch there. She asked if my agency would help her put together an author website to be ready for her book launch. Then she asked me to be the interviewer during the event and so I came up with a fun list of questions to ask her during the event. In addition, a guest speaker from the non-profit was part of her event and the whole thing was video recorded. The video was perfect for uploading to her website and for use as content on her social media.

Her book launch was a great example of how an independently published author put together a meaningful marketing event on a modest budget.

Digital Ads

The role of advertising in book selling has changed dramatically in the last several years. While many magazines and newspapers have disappeared, there are still printed and online options in many niches to consider. Television advertising has always been more the purview of traditional publishers for their biggest author names.

With the rise of Amazon's e-book publishing and sales platform, digital advertising has become more important to cut through the clutter and generate more sales. Here are some key things for digital ads to when promoting your book(s):

- For independently published authors, take an online course for the ways to create and place ads on Amazon, Facebook, or other social media. There are many courses and videos offered including "how to" webinars from Amazon, like their free **Amazon Ads for Authors**.[13]

- Check out YouTube videos on how to place ads as well as courses from pundits who specialize in helping authors.

- Determine a budget that you are willing to spend for training and for the actual ad campaign. Even on a small budget, you can simply test digital ads starting with as little as $5 a day on Facebook and set your own spend on Amazon.

- To get more sophisticated, a very successful independent author recommended paying for a course and she chose Mark Dawson's **Ads for Authors**[14] to set up her book and help with the launch.

- For setting up Facebook and Instagram campaign, consider the resources at other services like BookBaby where the minimum is $100 per week.[15]

One of the most important aspects of digital ads is the keywords and metadata you use for each campaign. In addition, remember to track the sales from the choices made in setting up the ad campaign. This will help you finetune future campaigns.

As an example, in 2022, I created a group called the Mysteries & More Marketing Network for the Sisters in Crime Grand Canyon Writers chapter. The idea was to have two work groups, one for aspiring authors and one for published authors, to explore marketing concepts for book sales. To make it more effective, there was homework to put the concepts to work for each group.

One participant decided to try using the "pay per click" ads at $5 per day to promote her newest book. When she tracked the results, it gave her a starting point and good information. She reported back to the group that she spent $100 on the campaign and made sales of $59. Because the sales did not pay for the ad cost with her first try, she brought the results to one of our meetings. We discussed how tweaks in keywords might help attract better sales. Another aspect we discussed was that increasing the frequency of campaigns with changing keywords would help to build better results.

3 ACTION STEPS:

1. What three things will you need to get more training on to promote your book?

2. Do a review of your online presence including your author business website and your author social media for being current.

3. Describe your perfect book launch and how it will be a success. Write down those things that you feel will enhance book sales.

CHAPTER 7
Your Promotional Campaign for Book Sales

The Magic of 7

When planning your marketing campaigns, it is important to consider the number of times it takes for a human brain to remember a name, product, brand, or logo. Attention spans have gotten so short with the immediacy of online news, updates, and social media, that the first time someone sees your marketing or social media, it may not register. In marketing textbooks, there is often a reference to how it takes seven times to create a position in the mind of a prospect or someone who has never seen your messaging before.

In preparing marketing plans, I have named this aspect the "Magic of 7." It is often overlooked but it is critical for authors to "touch" readers and potential readers at least seven times in the year. By building seven touches with your message, graphic or post, you have more chance to engage with the target reader and get a book sale.

The other important aspect to these touches is the consistency of the graphics, logo identity, and messages in all marketing materials and communications. The ongoing connection provides the means for establishing your brand identity in the reader's mind. The more touches that have your author brand, the easier it is for a target reader to remember you and your book(s).

To achieve the "Magic of 7," you need to make a commitment to regular touches of your author brand using emails, ads, and social media to be successful. Consider:

- Seven touches for each ad campaign.

- Seven touches through the year for retaining readers.

- Seven touches for a new book launch using emails.

- Seven touches for a backlist of already published books.

- Seven touches for a speaking gig or presentation.

- Seven touches for winning an award.

- Seven touches for anthology or short story publication.

- And many more!

If it takes me seven times to remember your name, author brand, genre, and book, you can use a mixture of monthly e-newsletters, social media posts, and digital ads. The key is to create a formula to fill out your schedule that is easy for you to maintain. For example, you can set up seven emails that focus on a book launch or seven social media posts that promote a backlist of your books.

Working on Your Strategies: 10 Tips to Keep in Mind

There are many ways to promote your book(s) and nothing is set in stone. As mentioned earlier, it's about your time, talent, and treasure. In essence, you will need to see how much time you are willing to spend to learn and create promotional strategies. And you will need to consider how much you want to spend. To get you started in building your marketing plan, here are some easy ideas to consider:

1. **Be easily recognizable**. Keep your image at the forefront by staying consistent with author brand colors and graphics on your website, social media, and email.

2. **Positioning is everything**. Create a tagline that identifies your author brand easily for readers. Successful published authors, like Hank Phillippi Ryan, may lead with their success which she does with "USA Today Best-Selling and Award-Winning Author,"[16] yet newer authors may use something like Raquel V. Reyes with her tagline of "Latina Sleuths."[17]

3. **Encourage your readers to provide reviews**. Ask for them online and through email to get reviews to use in your promotions.

4. **Alert prospects and readers to new projects**. Always include reminders of your upcoming book, or a story, as well as new projects because the marketplace is so jammed, they need to be told again and again.

5. **Develop an author table display.** Create a visual backdrop with a stand-up sign or poster using your author brand, tagline, and colors - perfect for book fairs or book launches in bookstores.

6. **Maximize your website for more impact of your author brand.** Use "happy reader" reviews, announcements, giveaways, and "how to purchase" links to get readers to visit your website often. These can be used in emails, social media and ad campaigns.

7. **Pay attention to the power of e-news**. Treat email newsletters as a conversation with a potential or target reader. Use fun snippets from your current book or series, "insider" information about your character, highlight other authors that write your genre, and/or a "sales" call at the bottom for the person to buy.

8. **Concentrate on showcasing your books**. Remember that the messages you create need to include asking the reader to purchase, yet not be the only message in the email or social media post.

9. **Make your author brand work for you.** Consistently sending the same graphics and messaging to make it easy for readers to identify your work will firmly establish your author brand in the mind of the target reader.

10. **Never assume the reader remembers**. Get your message in front of them as often as possible with the Magic of 7 formula.

Promotion

In marketing plans, most time is spent on the element of promotion to attract buyers. The promotion strategy includes advertising, e-marketing, social media, public relations, and personal selling. Each is meant as a layer to create a group of prospects that are ready to buy.

For promoting your books, here are a few ideas for each of these layers:

- **Advertising** – In today's market, most of the options are online from running digital ads on Amazon, social media, and book promotion sites. There are many online workshops to learn about effective ways to run ads because each medium has different nuances to consider.

- **E-Mail Marketing** – To gain access directly to a prospect or reader, a necessary aspect of book marketing is an email list. As a direct connection to family, friends, and readers, emails get different attention than social media. Think of it as part of your book's success to build your email address list while also creating good content. From fun story snippets to insider secrets in your book, to interesting tidbits about writing or motivation, make the email newsletters interesting to read. You can even ask questions of readers or encourage them to vote on a book cover or run a contest to win a book. Above all, make your e-news engaging and short.

- **Social Media** – Choose the ones that connect with your target reader and limit them to make the most of your content and time. The main apps are Facebook, Instagram, Twitter, and YouTube. Each of these platforms have billions of active users.[18] A recent addition is TikTok which has a subgroup called BookTok. While not as large as the other platforms, authors have found success in uploading videos to promote their books. Another social media option is Pinterest, an image-sharing platform. It does not have the same level of active users and is not as interactive without the updating feed. Overall, each platform has good aspects to reaching target readers and they all take your time. Pick one or two that you enjoy and can commit to being the most consistent in content creation of text, graphics, photos, and videos.

- **Public Relations** – There are lots of options to help get your book exposed to target readers including book signings, podcasts, blogs, readings in libraries or bookstores, and video or Zoom interviews. If you're with a traditional publisher, some of these will be set up for your book launch which is helpful and then you can promote the date(s). If indie-published, it is best to create a list of bookstores, libraries, bloggers, and podcasters that you will feel comfortable with being a guest.

- **Personal Selling** – For authors, the actual selling one-on-one comes during live opportunities such as book launch personal appearances at libraries, bookstores, and book fairs. In addition, you can find book conferences to be on a panel and bring some books. Another option is to promote to book clubs and attend either in person or by Zoom. Important for indie-published authors is to have books in hand with a payment vehicle like Square for taking credit cards, some cash and even Venmo or Apple Pay.

Trying New Outreach – Podcasts

In recent years, advances in technology have created new online options for reaching prospective readers. The increasing numbers of podcasts as well as the growth of video in the social media formats has given authors new ways to promote themselves and their books. For every author, the issue with being a guest on a podcast or Zoom, or creating a video is not easy. From prepping the type of subject that listeners will find interesting, to making sure you have good lighting for Zoom or video, preparation is key to giving you more confidence for your gust appearance.

Starting with podcasts, here are some interesting statistics:

- The number of podcasts was documented as over 2.5 million by October 2022. These are across many genres. Key is to find a few that fit your genre or type of story. Yet, with the high number of podcasts, you can narrow down who you contact for a guest spot to best fit your storyline as well as the age of the listeners.[19]

- As of 2022, 62% of those age 12+ in the U.S. (an estimated 177 million people) have ever listened to a podcast, up from 57% last year (2021). And, 90 million Americans are weekly podcast listeners.[20]

- While comedy is the most popular genre, there are many different types of podcasts in every genre. In the top 10, there are True Crime, Self Help, Investigative Journalism, and more. Yet, within these podcast genres, there are many different themes that may fit your writing or book(s).[20]

Many podcasts are focused on the craft and business of writing, yet you can expand your search to find podcasts that attract the listeners who would likely read your genre. With thousands of potentials, realize that the hosts are always looking for guests. You also may have an element in your story that relates to other podcast subjects. Find one that connects audiences with your book(s) such as a true crime podcast where you discuss how your detective novel resembles a true crime story. Or if you write historical fiction, to find podcasts that discuss the time period your book is set in. You might even talk about the value of writing on a self-help podcast and mention your book(s). Plus, it's free with the opportunity to put the link to your episode out in social media. Simply have a pitch ready to email the host when you find a podcast that attracts your target reader demographic as well as fits your genre and story.

The Visual Connection with Videos

Creating videos is a great way to visually bring your book(s) to life with prospects and readers. The incredible engagement of consumers of all ages on YouTube and TikTok with short entertaining videos has caused other social media platforms to add video to their platforms. Adding videos to your website and social media allows more connection to your readers, whatever age for your genre.

- **Establish a YouTube channel.** The reason to include YouTube in your marketing ideas is that it's the second most visited website after Google Search. It is the heavyweight in video online. YouTube now has more than a billion unique users every single month.[21]

- **Try using BookTok on TikTok.** While there has been a lot of concern over TikTok having Chinese owners, usage has soared, with 36% percent of those in the U.S. age 12+ currently using the social media service as of 2022. This is a 57% increase over 2021, placing it third for overall social media reach behind Instagram (46%) and Facebook (63%). Among those age 12-34, 61% use TikTok, second only to Instagram (72%). Among those age 35-54, TikTok now surpasses Pinterest, Twitter, Snapchat, and LinkedIn with 34% of those in the U.S. age 35-54 using TikTok.[22] There is fun content uploaded by authors using a special hashtag of #booktok identifies them for prospects and readers. A short, fun video can engage people with your author brand.

- **Using video content helps you capture that attention.** According to Animoto, 60% of consumers who made a purchase from a brand found out about them on social media.[23] While YouTube is still the grand master, many video options are available in the social media platforms. You can make shorter video clips to upload to Instagram, Facebook, LinkedIn, and Twitter. Be sure to provide a link to your website or where the person viewing the clip can buy your book.

Not everyone is comfortable with developing video content, yet there are many ways to do simple videos. First, you can use only graphics with your voice narrating. Second, a candid shoot with you talking directly into the camera. And third, a well-produced video of you being interviewed by another person and then using video editing. When in doubt, start with a quick, short video shot with your phone, even as a selfie, that does not require editing. This can be a relatable and fun way to engage with the viewer.

When setting up a live video recording, it is important to jot down an outline with maybe a short script. Make sure to test the lighting and use a ring light to soften the glare or enhance a dark room. Finally, wear solid, dark colors to keep the focus on your face and message. If you are not going to be live and only recording your voice over a book cover or other graphic, the key is to keep your voice slow and low.

10 Ideas for Video Marketing

If you are comfortable with creating videos, start a list of ideas. Think of what helps promote your author brand and book(s) from your phone, using Zoom or working a camera, here is a quick list that

I came up with for my mystery series:

1. Video introducing book.

2. Video to introduce each chapter of the book.

3. Video highlighting characters or people of interest in the book.

4. Video of reviews about the book.

5. Video to introduce the series.

6. Video to discuss a special aspect from each book.

7. Video to discuss using a different location or time in history.

8. Video discussing the book cover concept.

9. Video talking about the difficulties and benefits of writing the book.

10. Video reviewing other favorite books that inspired me.

Fun Exercise to Try: Develop 10 of Your Own

1. _____

2. _____

3. _____

4. _____

5. _____

6. _____

7. _____

8. _____

9. _____

10. _____

Prepping for In-Person Events

As a writer, you may not be comfortable with personally selling your book(s). Yet, you will have opportunities to be in front of audiences which is an opportune time to sell more books. The key is to be prepared to engage with prospects and readers alike.

When presenting a workshop or sitting on a panel, it is important to have a relevant topic, an outline of talking points, and a script or handout. If you're nervous about doing a workshop, consider creating a PowerPoint presentation to keep your thoughts organized and flowing well. Include your website address as well as links to buy your books.

If you're standing at a table at a book fair or conference, it is always good to have your business card with links to your books for an interested person to pick up if they are cruising through the event. Some authors prefer to hand out a bookmark, postcard, or flyer as an inexpensive "touch."

For more tips on presenting, the next chapter will provide ideas to promote your book from the stage.

A Note about Selling

When asked about selling, most people will answer that they are not good at it or hate it. The fear of rejection is acute with personal selling especially when the author is more introverted. Here is a great way to tackle personal selling of your books:

1. **Prepare the logline and elevator pitch** - Be prepared with a logline, a one-sentence summary or description of your book, to hook interest as you talk to someone and then follow up with the thirty-second elevator pitch using words that inspires you to smile as you describe the story.

2. **Talk fun benefits** - Shift to thinking of the benefits to your target reader that make you passionate about your book. Start a list of talking points that you are comfortable using to encourage a prospect or reader to buy your book(s).

3. **Use handouts** – If you are shy, having a physical item like a bookmark, small flyer or business card can help give you an opening to talk about what the other person likes to read.

3 ACTION STEPS:

1. Fill out the marketing schedule worksheet of those promotional mediums you want to use. Include the number, the timing, and the theme of each for the first quarter (three months) to get an idea of what it will mean for your marketing consistency using the Magic of 7 touches.

2. Try the video exercise to see what ideas you come up with to promote your book, stay in touch with readers, and sell more copies.

3. For attending conferences, book fairs, and other events, create your logline, elevator pitch and talking points to be ready to sell. Remember that loglines should be written as a clear, concise one-sentence teaser of your book to hook a target reader and your elevator pitch is a longer description of the important elements of your story when the person wants to know more.

Notes:

CHAPTER 8
Promoting Your Book from the Stage

Being Comfortable in Front of an Audience

As an author, you may have an opportunity to speak at a conference or sit on a panel. Organizations – whether they are made up of writers, readers, or the public – consistently look for speakers. Be ready to offer your topics as a speaker or to be a panelist.

You might be invited to speak to a writing group. Contact bookstores to offer to do an event such as a book signing, talk about your book, or a reading. A local library may have a book fair with opportunities to speak or to stand at a table to talk to readers.

The kicker is – most people have a fear of speaking in front of an audience. In fact, here is an interesting statistic:

"Glossophobia, or a fear of public speaking, is a very common phobia and one that is believed to affect up to 75% of the population. Some individuals may feel a slight nervousness at the very thought of public speaking, while others experience full-on panic and fear." [24]

Even though I have spoken in front of thousands of people, and presented hundreds of workshops and conferences, it still makes me nervous to step on stage. Once I have all my preparations ready, I do a bit of deep breathing to calm myself. Then when walk onto the stage, I'm prepared to give valuable information and calm enough to have fun at the same time.

If you have a fear of speaking, you can overcome nervousness and enjoy yourself with a few tips and tricks that have helped me be a speaking success.

Tips for Presentation Skills

Being in front of audiences as a speaker for conference keynotes, workshops, panels, book signings, and other live events is great for exposure to new target readers. You may also have opportunities on podcasts, in videos, or online in Zoom meetings. Here are a few tips on tackling speaking in front of audiences:

- **Memorize your logline and elevator pitch** - Be prepared with your logline of under ten words to hook the other person's interest and then follow up with the thirty-second elevator pitch using 30-50 words that describe the story.

  o *What's in the book that inspires you to smile when you talk to someone about it?*

- **Create a list of the reader benefits** – Have in mind a few reasons why your target reader will want to read your book. The target reader is more interested in the fun aspects of your story, including what made you so passionate about writing it.

  o *What genre does your book fit and those elements of your story that will engage readers of that genre?*

  o *Can you give three gems to pique interest as ideas of why people enjoy your book(s)? For example, is it a cozy mystery with no sex or violence?*

- **Use handouts** – Be prepared at any conference, panel, or online event to provide a list of key points in a PDF and include your contact information. If you are shy, having a physical item to hand out can help give you an effortless way to talk to new people. If the event is virtual, like an online webinar, Zoom meeting, or podcast, you can provide it to the host to send out or offer to email the PDF to the audience.

  o *Do you have your author brand on all your materials? Examples about how to buy your books can include a PDF handout, bookmarks, small flyers, and business cards.*

The Speaking Success Checklist

The key to stepping on a stage is to be comfortable, prepared, and confident. Many of my writer friends and business associates have joined a Toastmasters International Chapter or other training program to get rid of the jitters to be more successful.

The following is a list of tip sections will help you be your best during a presentation, a workshop, or sitting on a panel:

- **Be Prepared with Clear, Informative, and Short Answers**

- **Practicing Your Delivery – "6 Tips to Slow Your Speech"**

- **Overcoming Stage Fright: Tricks for Calming Nerves**

- **Onstage Preparation and Confidence**

- **Capturing Attention by Sensory Style**

You will find questions, tips, and new tools to consider when you want to enhance your presentation skills and feel comfortable in front of an audience. These elements from the Presentation Skills Checklist will help you get ready for any speaking appearance.

Be Prepared with Clear, Informative, and Short Answers

When you have an opportunity to speak at a conference, a meeting, a book signing, a reading, or be a guest on a podcast, prepare yourself by answering to these questions:

- ❑ How can you dazzle the target readers/audience?
- ❑ Do you know who will be interviewing you?
- ❑ Have you researched other people on stage, on the panel, or in the interview?
- ❑ Are you prepared to provide some questions that would be asked of you?
- ❑ Do you have a couple of questions to engage the audience?
- ❑ What can you do to make it easier for the reader to find your books?
- ❑ Do you have a flyer, bookmark, or business card to give out?

Key is to get comfortable with the others involved as well as how to tailor content for your speech, panel answers, and interview questions. It will give you more confidence to have the content readily in mind.

Practicing Your Delivery – 6 Tips to Slow Your Speech

When we are nervous, an unanticipated consequence is that we start talking faster. Some speakers find that nerves can speed their talk up and finish early. Yet, the key is to talk slow enough for the audience to grasp your content and be able to ask a question if they are confused or need clarification. Here are some tips for you to present well:

- When presenting or being interviewed:
  - ❑ Before you start, take five deep breaths, filling deep into the bottom of your lungs.
  - ❑ Pause to allow you to slow down and check the audience's reactions.
  - ❑ Ask questions to garner involvement with your ideas, tips, and content.
  - ❑ Involve the audience with a quick exercise that gives you a chance to breathe.
  - ❑ Use repetition to slow yourself when you realize you're speeding up.
- Prepare in advance:
  - ❑Study your favorite TV news person to notice their cadence, any gestures, and the level of their voice.

❑Watch other presenters at conferences or during an interview for how they maintain poise when not speaking – from sitting quietly, to eye contact, to limiting fidgeting.

❑ Practice pace by reading a paragraph at three different rates of speed – from quick to slow.

Using these techniques helps control the pace of your speaking when nerves get the better of you!

Overcoming Stage Fright: Tricks for Calming Nerves

Even famous personalities get nervous and here is confirmation: "Many famous people have suffered from glossophobia, including actors, politicians and even presidents. Some notable examples are Renée Zellweger, Nicole Kidman, Abraham Lincoln, Gandhi, Sigmund Freud, and Thomas Jefferson. At some point, they all mention actually going out of their way to avoid speaking in public."[25]

The fear of public speaking can be mitigated when you have something to distract the mind to calm yourself before you step on the stage.

• Limber your lips with the classic rhyme, "Peter Piper picked a peck of pickled peppers."

• Take several deep breaths and use slow exhales, counting to 10 in and out.

• Smile wide and then frown, exaggerating as you move from one expression to the other.

These tricks are fun and easy to remember. They can help everyone do their best when a speaking or interview opportunity presents itself.

Onstage Preparation and Confidence

Whether you are an introvert or an extrovert, walking onto a stage is intimidating to most people. Here are quick tips to help you be prepared to shore up your confidence.

❑ Dress for the role – my recommendation is always to dress up one level from the recommended attire for attendees. According to **indeed.com**[26], there are four common types of dress code; business formal, business professional, business casual, and casual. Because most conferences or workshops are "business casual," dress one level up in business professional, such as a suit or sportscoat for men and a suit or nice dress for women.

❑ Know your lines – practice makes perfect, and a cheat sheet does help with the key points you want to make. Another good idea when creating your presentation is to use the framework of a certain number of points, such as; "The Three Best Tips For…" or "The Five Mistakes to Avoid…" Then, make sure to circle back and emphasize those points as a recap at the end.

❑ Be calm and check your equipment before the start of the presentation – this includes testing the microphone, setting up your phone as a timer to stay on time, and checking that your slides or PowerPoint are ready. Using the clicker a few times to move your slides before you start will make you even more comfortable. If you are sitting on a panel, test the microphone. If you have received the questions prior to the session, have a cheat sheet ready with the key points or comments you want to make.

❑ Smile and make eye contact – show you are genuine and friendly. According to **VirtualSpeech.com**, eye contact gives the audience a sense of connection with your message.[27] It may be helpful to find a friendly face in the front rows. Hint: If it distracts you to look at others, then look at the back wall just slightly above the heads of the attendees because it looks like you're looking at the audience.

❑ Focus on the WIN-WIN – know that you are providing really good information for the group and having a great time doing it. The key is to create a presentation or come up with key points that you wish you had known earlier as you started writing. Or relate the mistakes you learned that you feel will help those in the audience to be more successful.

Capturing Attention by Sensory Style

There are three main sensory styles that we all use to communicate with others which are visual, audio, and kinetic. Of these three, each person has one that is most dominant.

The importance of knowing your own sensory style is that you will create your presentation with your dominant style. For example, you may be an "audio" who relies on what is said and heard. While a person who is a "visual" needs something to see to believe. A "kinetic" requires something to hold onto to hear and understand your message. If you only present in your dominant style, it may mean losing a bunch of people in your audience.

Prepare your presentation to reach all three sensory styles. Consider the following ideas.

- Visuals – to gain their attention, have something to show and tell. Create a PowerPoint presentation for a speaking gig. If sitting on a panel, bring something to hold up for them to see like your book cover.

- Audios – because you are giving a presentation or appearing on a panel, make sure you speak with sufficient volume. Be confident and upbeat. It's important to use your voice to present clear talking points for the audience to easily hear you.

- Kinetics – being dominated by the sense of touch to learn and understand, you will do well with handing out something for them to hold while listening to you. (Have a printed handout.)

Shown in the graphics on the next page, you will see the eye movements and word choices that reflect a person's dominant sensory style.

Kinesthetics
A Kinesthetic will move hers/his eyes…

Auditories
An Auditory will move hers/his eyes…

Visuals
A Visual will move hers/his eyes…

Side Right

Up Right

Down Right
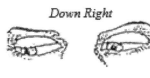

Side Left
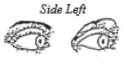

Up Left

Down Left
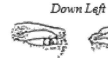

Defocused

Kinesthetic Words	Auditory Words	Visuals
	hear	see
	listen	look
feel	ring a bell	view
touch	tune in	picture
get a handle	tune out	perspective
grasp	on key	envision
touch base	tone	clear
make contact	tell	bright
hammer in	voice	foggy
get a hold on	state	appear
come to grips with	word for word	show
give me a hand	clear as a bell	short-sighted
keep in touch	loud and clear	tunnel vision
sharp	snap to it	in light of
smooth	manner of speaking	well-defined

Eye movement and the words we choose reflect our dominant sensory style used to listen, participate, and learn. Being able to understand sensory styles helps you connect better with your audiences and target readers!

3 ACTION STEPS

1. What topic (or several topics) do you have experience with, enjoy researching, or feel comfortable offering to speak on?

2. Write an outline for one topic that would interest an audience. Using a title such as, "Here Are Three Tips For…" is a great way to start.

3. What sensory style are you? Make sure you include ways to reach the other styles as well with a good script for audios, a set of presentation slides for visuals, and a handout for the kinetics to hold onto that helps them listen to your message!

Notes:

CHAPTER 9
Content Marketing Tips to Build Your Outreach

Creating Content to Engage

As a writer, you have the creative foundation to develop content for emails and social media to promote your book(s) and how you describe your author brand. Yet, your time is often focused on writing great stories rather than worrying with business stuff like marketing.

The key to making it easier to create content is to repurpose what you have in your files that will engage your target reader. The posts and messages can range from updates on a new project, events where you will be selling books or having a book signing, and book launch dates. In addition, let your target readers learn more about you as a writer with snippets of your life. Other ideas include reviews of your book(s) as well as reviews of other author's books that are in your genre you believe the readers may enjoy. If you have a hobby such as taking photos of flowers, landscapes, or animals, these can be used as insights into you as the person, not just as an author.

In addition, if you have a blog or podcast, you can use snippets within emails, as a tweet, and as uploads on Instagram and Facebook. For those who like to create videos, every social media format is offering some form of short or longer videos. An example of a newer favorite is BookTok on the social media platform, TikTok. Through short videos, authors have been able to engage a broader audience to sell more books.

Unlock the Power of Content Repurposing

There are some things to consider for building content in a quick and easy way. Content repurposing allows you to breathe new life into your existing material, reach a wider audience, and drive greater engagement. Let's explore the benefits of content repurposing with some actionable tips.

- **Reinforce Your Brand Messaging** – Consistency is key when it comes to building a strong author brand. Use consistent branding elements, such as the same typeface for your name/pseudonym, colors, and tagline to create a cohesive brand experience for your audience. This familiarity builds trust and strengthens your brand's recognition, ultimately boosting your marketing efforts.

- **Extend Your Content's Lifespan** –Repackage an email newsletter into a series of bite-sized social media posts. Try making a video book trailer on Canva and upload it to your YouTube channel. Develop a graphic of your book cover with the link to the video channel to post across your social media accounts. Consider transforming an insightful blog post into an engaging infographic which is an image that shows your information minimized into bar graphs, pie charts, line charts, or network diagrams. In essence, condense your information into an interesting visual which has a link to read the whole post on your website. The key is to maximize the content you create to maintain a consistent presence across different platforms.

Content Ideas to Repurpose:

1. Email Article
2. Book Cover
3. Blog Post
4. Short Story
5. First Chapter
6. Character Description
7. Photos
8. Book Review
9. Representative Graphic
10. Interview with Author

- **Reach New Audiences** – People consume content in different ways. Some read blogs, while others enjoy watching videos or listening to podcasts. In addition, each person has her/his own preference in social media. Others enjoy Instagram more than Twitter or Facebook rather than BookTok. Since it is hard to cover every social media platform as well as blogs, video production and more, you need easy ways to slice and dice your content. You can tell a story about one of your characters in an email and then create a photo representation of the same character to put up on Instagram with a link to your website to read the story. The idea is to engage with target readers across various platforms to also attract new audiences.

- **Boost Engagement on Social Media** – While you may have a preferred social media channel you enjoy, to build and engage your target reader and fan base, you need to show up on as many as possible. It is about taking a larger piece of your marketing or book content and adapting it to a variety of formats. As an example, start with a blog post or email newsletter for content and then slice and dice it into smaller pieces for every social media platform. You can use a book cover graphic to post on Twitter, Instagram, and Facebook. Then, use Zoom or your phone to record yourself reading the first chapter for a captivating YouTube video. If you know how to use a video editing app or program, you can trim that same video down to upload on BookTok, Instagram and Facebook reels of short videos.

- **Improve Showing Up on Searches**– A final thought on repurposing content is that many authors are not familiar with how to show up in more Google or Amazon searches. Across the internet, search engines value fresh and relevant content. By repackaging your content into different formats and distributing it across various platforms, you increase your chances of appearing in search engine results for a wider range of keywords. This expanded visibility is known as Search Engine Optimization (SEO) and understanding the value gives you the ability to drive organic traffic to increase book sales.

Content repurposing is a powerful strategy that allows you to maximize the value of your existing content, reach new audiences, and enhance your marketing and social media efforts. By repackaging your content into different formats, you can extend its lifespan, improve SEO, boost engagement on social media, and reinforce your brand messaging. Embrace the versatility of your content and unlock its potential by repurposing it wisely.

Get creative, experiment with different formats, and watch as your content works harder for you, generating greater visibility, engagement, and ultimately, driving your marketing success to sell more books.

More Slicing and Dicing Content

When it comes to repurposing content for social media, there are several effective ways to slice and dice one piece of content into various posts. Here are some ideas to help you maximize the potential of your content across different social media platforms:

- **Snippets and Quotes**: Extract key insights, statistics, or impactful quotes from your original content. Create visually appealing graphics using tools like Canva or Adobe Spark and share them as standalone posts on platforms like Instagram, Facebook, Twitter, or LinkedIn. These snippets can serve as teasers, capturing attention and encouraging users to engage with your content.

- **Infographics**: As mentioned earlier, consider creating a chart of your characters, key settings, symbols of the era the story is set in, or plot. Infographics are highly shareable as a graphic file in email and on all your social media platforms like Instagram, Facebook, Pinterest, or Twitter. They are great for providing a quick overview of your book in an easily digestible format to intrigue and hook a target reader.

> **Easy Content Example**
>
> Develop a blog post with an eye-catching fun photo or graphic.
> - The post is first used on your **blog**.
> - Mention the blog post subject in an **email** with a link to the post.
> - The beginning line can be used on **Twitter** with the graphic and a link to the post.
> - The photo or graphic can be used on **Instagram** to link to the post.
> - A short version of the blog post can be used on **Facebook** with the graphic.
> - Read the blog post in a video to upload to **YouTube**.

- **Step-by-Step Guides or Tutorials**: If your content includes a step-by-step process or tutorial, break it down into individual steps and create separate posts for each step. Share them as a series on Instagram, Facebook, or Twitter. Use visually appealing images or videos to accompany each step and provide concise explanations or tips to keep users engaged.

- **Behind-the-Scenes Content**: If your original content includes any behind-the-scenes information or experiences, share snippets or photos that give your audience a glimpse into your creative process or workspace. This type of content is particularly popular on platforms like Instagram Stories, Facebook Stories, or Snapchat, where you can share more informal and authentic updates.

- **Video Teasers or Summaries**: With cell phones having video capability, you can film yourself to create short video clips or teasers. Consider highlighting special insights into your main character or villain or other characters to interest the viewer in reading the book. These videos can be shared on platforms like Instagram Reels, BookTok/TikTok, or Twitter. Keep them concise and visually engaging, encouraging viewers to seek out the full content for more information. There are more suggestions for the video in Chapter 12.

- **Question and Answer Sessions**: Take questions from your audience related to your content and create separate posts answering those questions. You can do this through written posts, images with text overlays, or short video clips. This approach allows you to address specific concerns or interests of your audience while promoting your original content.

- **User-Generated Content**: Encourage your audience to engage with your original content and share their experiences or opinions related to it. Repurpose their comments, testimonials, or reviews as social media posts. This not only showcases social proof but also encourages further engagement and interaction from your audience.

Remember to tailor the content format and messaging to suit each social media platform's requirements and preferences. Adapt the content to fit the character limits, visual guidelines, and engagement features specific to each platform. You will find more information online at Instagram Help Center[28], Facebook Help Center[29], Twitter Help Center[30], or YouTube.[31]

By repurposing your content in these ways, you can provide value to your audience across multiple social media channels and maximize your reach and engagement.

Make the Most of a Content Schedule

To put together marketing activities for the year, in Chapter 5 on page 34, a handy calendar worksheet was introduced to capture your content ideas. It helps to prevent wasting lots of time every week trying to throw something together to put out in social media or in an e-newsletter.

Using the worksheet, below is a simple example of documenting your marketing projects with the medium, the working title or theme of the content, and a place to note if it was accomplished. The final item would be a "Notes" column to document results or changes needed in the future. As a tool, the worksheet offers a way to organize your thoughts and track the execution.

Month:

Date	Project Book, Series, Short Story, Launch, Other	Medium Email, Website, Blog, Social Media, Events, etc.	Working Title	Done Y/N	Notes

Here is an example of starting a Book Marketing Content & Schedule:

Date	Project Book, Series, Short Story, Launch, Other	Medium Email, Website, Blog, Social Media, Events, etc.	Working Title	Done Y/N
7-Oct	Fall Book Launch - First Wave	Email for Preorder	Discover a New Amateur Detective	
		Website - subscribe for free chapter and to Preorder	Be First to Get the New Book	
		Social Media - Book Cover with Offer Link	You Can Preorder Now	
14-Oct	Fall Book Launch - Second Wave	Email with first chapter offer & upcoming event	Get Ready to Talk Murder at (Event)	
		Social Media with event details	Mark Your Calendar	
21-Oct	Halloween Special Offer	Email - $0.99 Offer	Meet the new sleuth now for only $.99	

Email Basics to Market Your Book or Series

First, you need to start an email list and continue to work at building it. The concept of reaching out to target readers and your fan base is that email is a direct connection. Social media is hit or miss, but you know that an email is delivered to a specific inbox.

As a starter, friends and family are perfect to include and try out your email content. As a writing business, it is best to set up an account with a provider like Mailer Lite, MailChimp, Constant Contact or another service. The reason for these providers is the ease of use, multiple templates, and the ability to grow your database of email addresses. Plus, you will be able to get statistics to help you make better decisions such as if all of your emails are getting delivered, how many are opened, or how many people clicked on a link you put in the email. In addition, the service will help you with a form for people wanting to unsubscribe.

To attract more email subscribers, add a sign-up form on your website. Then as visitors sign up, you will need to create a welcome series. The first email is to thank the person for joining your list. Describe what to expect in terms of how often they will receive an email from you and the type of content. Some authors set up at least three follow-up email messages to be more engaging from the start. The second email can be one that offers a free first chapter of your book as a new subscriber. The third email might be a question about another book the person is reading. The idea is not to try and sell books right away. You can add links to buy your books at the bottom of the email.

A way to uncover more subscribers is to encourage social media followers to click the link to your website sign-up form. The use of demographics (age, gender, income level interests, etc.) that best describe your target reader can be used to customize ads in Facebook or Instagram. The social media posts will then appear in target reader feeds and your ad will encourage them to visit your website.

Writers often ask what content to put in their emails to make them more interesting for people to open and read. The goal is to have subscribers look forward to your emails, open them and read your message. One important consideration is how short people's attention spans are as they flip through their email on phones or laptops. A study from Microsoft Corp., cited in a Time magazine article, found people now generally lose concentration after eight seconds compared to a goldfish whose attention span is nine seconds.[32]

Ergo, keep your emails short. If you have a long article, give just the first paragraph or two in the email and link to "read more" on your website.

What should you try for content? You need to engage with your target readers and fan base, which requires interesting content.

Here is a list from our email worksheet:

- Offer a quiz.

- Ask a question.

- Give "How to" ideas.

- Book recommendation/review.

- Provide a favorite quote.

- Share a personal story.

- Try a quick test of knowledge.

- Offer a retro reference (i.e. Throwback Thursday).

- Snippet from a work in progress (WIP).

- Talk about favorite books, stories, and movies.

- Offer a free chapter.

- Publish a short story in segments.

Because you are a busy writer, a good tip is to develop your editorial calendar for content ideas and mediums to use for a month or more. Listing what you are going to do in the next month or several months allows you to remember to check the "Magic of 7" touches from Chapter 7. As a reminder, it takes seven times for us to remember a message or a brand.

Next Level Email Tips for Moving Forward

It is important to review your email results to make sure you are engaging subscribers to click through to your website or to order your book(s). It is important to check activity to see if you need to rework or enhance your efforts.

Here are some questions that will help you to review and organize your email strategy for more success:

- Who can I tap to join my email list?

- How can I use email before my novel is finished/printed?

- Who can I target to grow my email list?

- How can I test my email to see if it's working and measure results?

- When offering a freebie, how many people responded?

- As my book is published, has email increased book sales?

- What response did I get when offering a quiz or question?

- Did people click to visit my website?

- Did subscribers use the link provided to buy my book(s)?

As you might notice in your personal inbox, you get so many emails that you are often drawn to your favorites first. These are your favorites because they offer you something special or interesting tidbits that you find valuable.

Here are a few tips to enhance your email messages and increase interest form your target readers:

- Make sure all recipients have opted-in to receive your emails.

- Send your campaign from a good Internet Provider (IP) address like an email service that helps keep your email from being blacklisted.

- Use only 6 to 10 words in your subject lines that are truthful and informative yet tempt the target reader to open the email.

- Personalize subject lines with the reader's name.

- Use a recognizable sender's name.

- If using an email service provider, check how your email campaigns will look on mobile devices with their tools.

The email service providers offer video tutorials for you to learn more about how to best use their service for your email campaigns.

Final Email List-Building Idea

An excellent way to build your email marketing is to consider asking other authors or writing buddies to swap email lists. The idea is to give the other person your email content with links to your website. Then, you send that person's email message to your list with an introduction. Make sure that the other author or writing friend writes in the same genre. That way you both will benefit from adding new emails to your lists.

To maximize the benefit of the swap, be sure to:

- Create a freebie or lead magnet as an incentive for someone on the other author's list to sign up for your email list.

- Make sure your welcome series is set up to engage with the new target readers who do sign up from the other author's list.

- Check to see if the new subscriber clicks through to your book information and if anyone buys your book(s).

Email Marketing Checklist

See how email can be used to market your book or series:

Email Basics

- ☐ Build a List – Start with friends and family
- ☐ Set Up Email System – Mail Chimp/Constant Contact/Others
- ☐ Add a Sign-Up Form on Website – Capture email subscribers
- ☐ Create a "Welcome" message – Describe what to expect in timing, content, and your work
- ☐ Find Target Reader Audience - Age, geographic area and/or income level
- ☐ Develop an Editorial Calendar – List date and content ideas

Content Ideas

- ☐ Offer a quiz
- ☐ Ask a question
- ☐ Give fun "How to" ideas
- ☐ Book recommendation/review
- ☐ Provide a favorite quote
- ☐ Share a personal story
- ☐ Try a quick test of knowledge

- [ ] Offer a fun retro reference (Throwback Thursday)
- [ ] Snippet from a work in progress
- [ ] Talk about favorite books, stories, and movies
- [ ] Offer a free chapter
- [ ] Publish a story in segments

Questions to Consider

- [ ] Who can I tap to join my email list?
- [ ] How can I use email before my novel is finished/printed?
- [ ] Who can I target to grow my email list?
- [ ] How can I test my email to see if it's working and measure results?
- [ ] When offering a freebie, how many people responded?
- [ ] If you have published, does email increase book sales?
- [ ] What activity did you get when offering a quiz or question?
- [ ] If you gave a link to your website, did people visit?

Execution Tips

- [ ] Make sure to have an opt-in form on your website
- [ ] Offer an unsubscribe link in every e-news or email message
- [ ] Use 6 to 10 words in your subject lines to get the best open rate
- [ ] Send your email campaigns during the work day and after lunch
- [ ] Use a recognizable sender's name/email address

3 ACTION STEPS

1. If you have not started an email list, send an email to friends and family to jumpstart it. If you already have a list, try a low-cost Facebook ad mentioned above to offer something to attract new sign-ups on your website.

2. To maintain consistency for success in your email marketing, website, and social media, set up a calendar spreadsheet. List content ideas and weekly writing schedule to generate posts or articles for just one month. See how it goes and adjust to make it work best for you and your writing schedule.

3. Commit to an email list swap with another author or writer friend.

Notes:

CHAPTER 10
Positioning Yourself for Ongoing Success

Evaluating Results

For every author, whether traditionally or indie published, it is important to have a system in place to market your book or series. One successful indie author says she works on her marketing activities about 1.5 hours per day to promote launching new book(s) and a backlist of over 10 fiction novels. In addition, her marketing budget has grown to over $1,500 - $2,000 per month, which generates book sales revenue of more than six figures every year.

Once you have your initial marketing in place, the important next step is to evaluate the results to know what promotions, mediums, and messaging that are generating responses. To make the best decisions, here are some ideas of what to track:

- First, your marketing budget can be matched against the dollar amount of book sales for the year. The key is to see if the marketing efforts have generated a positive bottom line. If your promotions and communication efforts have netted a large number of book sales, then check that your marketing budget is fully covered. If the book sale numbers are barely covering or did not cover the marketing budget, you will need to review your promotions, ads, and emails to see how to improve results next year. Then, year over year, you can make better decisions regarding what to spend your budget to improve results to sell more books.

- Next, review your email marketing and website analytics to determine if people have visited your website and signed up using your online form. In addition, verify if using a lead magnet did acquire more sign-ups. It is important to keep a count of what email addresses you were able to attract and what seemed to trigger people to sign up.

- Finally, while digital ad campaigns do cost money, there is real value in popping up in a target reader's social media feed or on Amazon. Be sure to track the number of clicks from those ads to your website or sales page(s). Also, after running the ads, the number of books sold with dollar volume can be matched to the ad budget to see if the ads were able to generate enough book sales revenue to make them a winning strategy.

As a way to determine the value of those items that cost you money like running ads to sell books, you can use the following Cost Recovery worksheet. The commission paid either by a publisher or the amount paid from Amazon for e-books, can be the measuring stick for future campaigns.

In the following example, you can determine what it will take in sales to recover an ad campaign cost. Key is to use your entire marketing budget to see what it will take in book sales, whether traditionally or independently published, to recover an annual marketing investment.

Without checking to see what book sales volume you will need; it may seem that any dollar amount seems risky. So, using your current book price, use the Cost Recovery worksheet to figure out the level of book sales you need to recover what you spent on your marketing budget. Through the year, knowing this amount will help you determine if the marketing cost and promotional efforts are working.

Cost Recovery

Marketing Event		Approximate cost		
	Design of ad	0		
	Ad campaign cost	$50		
	TOTAL Marketing cost	$50		

Projected Marketing Cost Recovery: Estimated Number of Book Sales Needed

Product	Marketing Costs	Average Commission Rate	Book Sales Dollar Volume Needed to recover marketing costs (marketing cost/avg int rate)	Anticipated Average Amount per Book	Anticipated Number of Books to Recover Marketing Costs
Book - Traditional	$50.00	10.00%	$500	$10	50
Book - Self Published	$50.00	40.00%	$125	$10	13

Actual Marketing Cost Recovery - Book Sales Volume Achieved

Product	Marketing Costs	Average Commission Rate	Book Sales during ad campaign	Recovered Marketing Costs (book sales volume x margin)	Marketing Cost Recovery (Commission less marketing cost/)
Book - Traditional	$50.00	10.00%	$0	$0	($50.00)
Book - Self Published	$50.00	40.00%	$0	$0	($50.00)

The best thing is the execution of your marketing plan – from digital ads to social media to email marketing – will generate book sales. The worksheet will help identify those things that are the most successful as you review the sales as well as give you the confidence to do more of them. Continuing to execute the plan and reviewing results allows you to be more successful with each new marketing expenditure.

Overall, this exercise will give you confidence to continue adding more dollars to your marketing budget to fuel more book sales.

Digital Ad Campaign Results

As you begin to try digital ad campaigns to draw interest, attract more readers, and increase book sales, the key is to determine if the campaign actuall1y sells books. This is important from the moment you first put your toe in the water. Here is an easy worksheet to track results. And the worksheet allows you to keep making decisions about different keywords in Amazon or test social media audience demographics for sales.

Ad Campaign	Dates of Campaign	Keywords	Bid/Cost per Ad	Total Spend	No. of Impressions	Clicks	No. Sold	Sale Price per book	Total Sales ($)
Cozy Mystery Launch	June 1 - June 14	Let Amazon choose	$ 1.50	$ 50.00	17,201	56	9	$ 7.99	$ 71.91

Ongoing Checklist

As a writer, it is key to stay on your writing schedule to create a good novel, novella, or short story. Yet, duty calls to keep your marketing fresh. Here is a helpful checklist of important promotional content to develop, review, and update regularly:

Book Basics - Keep Updating

☐ Brief Description of Book – Logline with title and genre.

☐ Book Blurb – Brief 100–150-word statement to hook the reader.

☐ Reviews – From known authors or beta readers.

☐ Book Cover – Designed or mockup with colors to indicate genre.

☐ Target Audience – What are the specifics for age, geographic area, interests, gender, and/or income level who will enjoy your book(s).

☐ Audience Online – Websites, social media groups, blogs, podcasts, or book clubs that review books in your genre.

Branding

- [ ] Author Bio
- [ ] Author Photo
- [ ] Author tagline and typeface logo
- [ ] Purchased domain of your author name for website
- [ ] Blog name & description of content
- [ ] Links to social media [ ] Facebook [ ] Instagram [ ] Twitter [ ] BookTok

Marketing medium(s) for Promotion

- [ ] Professional Website - include author typeface logo and brand colors
- [ ] Amazon Book Page – for guidance see www.author.amazon.com/home
- [ ] Amazon Author Page – for guidance see www.author.amazon.com/home
- [ ] Email list – decide on email provider service and upload addresses
- [ ] Email list sign-up form on website
- [ ] Bookmark – printed with your author brand and promoting your book(s)
- [ ] Book Trailer – video to promote your book uploaded on YouTube or website
- [ ] Book Flyer – designed printed piece to hand out
- [ ] Digital Ads, Online Marketing – Facebook, Instagram, Amazon and others
- [ ] Social Media – Author Brand on Facebook, Instagram, YouTube, Twitter, and BookTok

Content

- [ ] Reader Reviews – Keep these handy for content and on website.
- [ ] Lead Magnets – Free item given for email sign-up like a chapter or short story.
- [ ] Pitch for Podcasters – Develop topic to talk about with the host.
- [ ] Blog Posts – Use for e-newsletters.
- [ ] Topic for speaking gigs – Create topic list for presentations.
- [ ] Social Media – Posts across all platforms.

3 ACTION STEPS

1. Using the budget that you plan to implement for your marketing, calculate a cost recovery to see how many books you will need to sell to break even. Try adjusting the numbers to determine what you feel comfortable using for the upcoming year.

2. Review how to use book ads on Amazon at:
   https://advertising.amazon.com/library/guides/advertising-books-on-amazon-authors   and check out their tutorials on ads here:
   https://advertising.amazon.com/solutions/industries/book-ads.

3. Select three things on the checklist that you need to include in your marketing plan going forward.

Notes:

CHAPTER 11
20-Minute Author Marketing Audit

While sometimes you can jump right into new projects, building a marketing plan is easier if you use an audit first. Examining where you are right now can identify the key elements you should begin working on to move forward.

Step One: Reviewing Current Efforts

Pull together everything you have used or created for marketing your book(s) – business cards, posters, and flyers. Then, print out your online accounts such as pages of your website, social media accounts, and e-mails sent to your target reader list. Remember, anything used to communicate with target readers is something that represents your brand. If you are a visual, tape them on a wall or white board at eye level to get a good look. Ask yourself the following questions and jot the answer that most often applies.

Always = 3   Almost Always = 2   Sometimes = 1   Never = 0

1. Does the description I have now of the target reader still apply to the person who will want to read my book(s)?

2. Is the image I presented to target readers consistent across all marketing elements to help target reader remember my author brand?

3. Are the colors of my author brand the same across all pieces for easy recognition of my name/pen name?

4. Did I create a document with details of my author brand colors, tagline, typeface, and graphics? Do they create a powerful and memorable image?

5. Is there an author brand tagline that speaks to the advantage of why target readers will enjoy reading my book(s)? If so, what is it?

6. Has the author brand tagline been included in every piece of my marketing communication (i.e., emails, flyers, business cards, blog, etc.)?

> I don't think anyone is ever writing so that you can throw it away. You're always writing it to be something. Later, you decide whether it'll ever see the light of day. But at the moment of its writing, it's always meant to be something. So, to me, there's no practicing; there's only editing and publishing or not publishing.
>
> **Steve Martin*** [33]

7. Will target readers find my website easily? Is it obvious it is my "writing business office" with contact information, where to buy my book(s), and sign up for my email list?

8. Is it easy for prospective readers to find links to buy my book(s) on my website, as well as in emails and within social media?

9. Do I keep my website updated to make sure target readers see timely information about my new book(s), launch activities, events, and other items that will engage them?

10. Have I created a budget to develop high quality and consistent marketing promotions?

Step Two: Scoring Your Efforts

Review your marketing materials once again and see if they match what you just answered. Since people need seven exposures to a name or message to remember it, examine how consistent your image is across all of them. Then add up the numbers associated with each answer to get your score.

If your score is:

- **25 -- 30** Wow, you are definitely protecting your author brand for the most consistency and increasing your name recognition for more book sales.

- **19 - 24** You're doing a good job of using your marketing to build your writing business.

- **13 - 18** Average use of your image, but more consistency would benefit your sales. You can use some fine-tuning to maximize results.

- **8 - 12** Low use of your image which may appear confusing to target readers. Time for an overhaul of your marketing efforts.

- **0 - 7** Below average on marketing your author brand. Make a fresh start by reviewing the earlier chapters.

Finally, Distill Your Ideas

This audit is most worthwhile when you can pull some new ideas and goals from the review. Doing this simple exercise is an investment in time and energy that really pays off for both you and your writing business!

Limit yourself to three things that you can do immediately to enhance your author brand and marketing efforts. Plug these into your budget and calendar. Then, consider three long-term goals you would like to achieve in the next 2-3 years.

What are 3 things you can do immediately to enhance your author marketing?

1.

2.

3.

What are 3 long-term goals regarding your author marketing that you would like to strive for to enhance your writing success?

1.

2.

3.

It's About Gaining Traction

The current competitive marketplace is daunting whether you are traditionally or independently published. Many traditionally published authors believe that the publisher will market their book(s). However, beyond the initial launch with some public relations assistance, it seems ongoing marketing has become the responsibility of the author. Many publishers want to know what kind of established platform an author has in email and social media before even signing her/him. Then, if the author does not engage with target readers to help drive book sales, if sales are weak, the publisher will drop the author's contract.

For an independently published author, the entire sales process falls on your shoulders. Merely uploading an e-book to Amazon will not attract sales due to the millions of books that are available. You must use the marketing plan, set a budget, and develop promotional tools to get in front of target readers who will buy your book(s).

12 Ideas for Book Marketing checklist

1. Author brand statement with a description of who are you as a writer, what genre you write and why you love to write.
2. Create three blog posts, short stories, or flash fiction as a cache of quick content.
3. Set up an email through Google as a gmail.com account.
4. Secure your name as a domain name for website at GoDaddy and sign up for their simple website using WordPress.
5. Establish an author website – Include tabs for About, Books, Contact, Blog, Freebie.
6. Add a form to "Subscribe to my updates/e-news" to capture email addresses.
7. Develop a freebie to give to someone who signs up for updates.
8. Create a schedule to follow for updates/e-news for next 3 months or longer.
9. Gather email addresses from your Outlook or other email program as starter for your author brand.
10. Set up account with MailerLite, Mailchimp, Constant Contact or other email service provider.
11. Add social media accounts for your author brand.
12. Set up a Zoom account for future "meet the author" or recording videos about your writing.

Therefore, for both traditionally and independently published authors, all the marketing efforts you can do to build and protect a consistent author brand and engage with target readers will enhance your book sales and professional image as well.

3 ACTION STEPS

1. Complete the audit and list the 3 ideas to do immediately. Calendar these to do in the next two to three months.

2. Determine if you need to create a budget to achieve these 3 ideas.

3. Then, review your 3 long-term goals (2-3 years) and make notes about what it will take to implement them. Write down the time, talent, and treasure to accomplish them. The key is to gain the scheduling across the next year and a budget of the funds you will need.

CHAPTER 12
Help with Next Steps

Congratulations on your commitment to making your dreams come true and achieving the success you want by developing an author brand and a marketing plan. Both will enhance your book sales!

When you are ready to stretch a little further, here are some next level steps to consider. The variety of options and providers that you can use relies on three things:

- **Marketing Plan** – Once you have the basics covered, do you have the time to manage more elements?

- **Marketing Budget** – Can you add more financial resources to increase marketing efforts to enhance sales?

- **Your Expertise** - Are you willing to learn new things or ability to hire someone who can handle the additional marketing efforts for you?

An author friend started her career writing thrillers and was fortunate to get a three-book contract with a major imprint. She was excited to be traditionally published, and then the imprint shut down. While she continued to receive a few royalties from the publisher, it was not enough to put her two kids through college. The idea she uncovered was to write romance novellas under a pseudonym, publish them herself, and sell them on Amazon.

To get started with a target reader list, she did email swaps with other indie romance writers. Her goal was to publish several books a year to increase her income.

Within one year, she was making more in one month from the sales of her independently published books than she received in royalties from the traditional publisher for her thrillers in an entire year. She was also able to get the rights back for the trio of novels from her previous publisher. She re-released her backlist of original thrillers to add to the romances, and with her new strategy, she was able to earn a mid-six-figure annual income.

As mentioned in Chapter 11, another author friend has always been independently published and worked on marketing and advertising to build sales of her first series which made over half a million dollars. She continues to make mid-six figures each year. Interestingly, one of her novellas was made into a Hallmark holiday movie. Recently, another production company bought the rights to a different book to create a television series.

The key to both of these successful authors is that they write good quality stories, and equally important, they implement a consistent marketing plan each year.

Questions from Published and Aspiring Authors

Throughout this handbook, you have a variety of steps you can take to develop your author brand and a marketing system to generate the book sales you want to achieve. As you learn what works best for you, your time, and your budget, there are often more questions that pop up for what is next.

From writer friends and participants in the Mysteries & More Marketing Network that I lead, below are some insightful questions. The answers will give you additional resources to help you move forward with marketing for more book sales.

Marketing Plan & Budget

What is the best practice for creating an author brand marketing plan – annual, six months or quarterly?

Creating an effective author marketing plan involves focusing on several key steps. Here's a quick reference guide:

- **Define your goals**: Establishing clear goals will help you tailor your marketing strategies accordingly – as well as give you the timeline for the plan. By clarifying marketing objectives, your plan will be focused on issues such as aiming to increase book sales, building your author brand, or expanding your reach beyond the existing readership.

- **Identify your target audience**: Remember that not everyone is your target reader. The ability to consider factors such as age, gender, whether employed or retired, other interests, and genre preference helps to tailor your marketing content to reach the right prospects.

- **Develop your author brand:** Your brand is how readers perceive you and your work. As noted in Chapter 7, it takes seven contacts for your messaging to be remembered by your target reader. Having the same name, colors, typeface, and tagline builds consistency for your author brand across all your marketing efforts.

- **Build the elements of your author platform**: To engage with readers and build a community around your work, elements in your marketing plan and budget should include:

- **Author website**: As your "office" for your writing business, a professional website is the place where people get information about your books, your author bio, complete an email sign-up form, and learn where to buy your books or contact you.

- **Social media**: Identify the social media platforms where you believe your target audience is most active. Build a presence on those platforms and regularly share updates, engage with readers, and promote your work.

- **Email marketing**: You can use social media to drive prospects to your website to sign up for your email list. Then connect with interested readers through newsletters, exclusive content, and book updates.

- **Leverage book reviews and endorsements**: Positive reviews and endorsements can significantly impact your book's success. Reach out to book bloggers, influential readers, and book review websites to request reviews. Also, consider seeking endorsements from well-known authors or influencers in your genre.

- **Utilize online book promotion platforms**: Take advantage of online book promotion platforms, such as BookBub, BookFunnel, Goodreads, and LibraryThing, to promote your books to a wider audience. These platforms offer various promotional opportunities, including author profiles, book giveaways, advertising, and author events.

- **Find ways to engage with your target readers**: Building genuine connections with your target readers will foster loyalty and word-of-mouth promotion. Regularly watch over your social media platforms to reply to comments. Set up book events and signings at bookstores and libraries. Attend book fairs and conferences that fit your genre and offer connections with readers.

- **Plan marketing campaigns**: The idea of marketing campaigns is to create content to reach a specific audience effectively such as:

- **Paid advertising**: Utilize online advertising platforms, such as Facebook Ads or Amazon Advertising, to target specific reader demographics and promote your books.

- **Content marketing**: Create a themed campaign to promote your book(s), to launch a book or special offer across platforms to attract and engage readers. The key is to include the same theme, matching graphics and messaging across your social media, website, and email.

- **Book events**: Organize or participate in book signings, author panels, literary festivals, and other events to connect with readers, gain exposure, and sell books. With the use of your social media, email list and website, get the word out about where target readers can meet you.

- **Regularly analyze results**: At least quarterly, make sure to evaluate the effectiveness of your marketing efforts. Most website providers have analytics tools to measure website traffic and give you who is clicking through to your website as well as signing up for your email list. In addition, most of the social media platforms have information on engagement or find out more in their Help Centers. The email service provider will have tools to check on email open rates to see if readers were interested enough to fully open the email as well as if anyone clicked through on links in the email.

Finally, include the marketing cost recovery with book sales achieved. Reviewing results compared to costs allows you to identify what's working well and adjust your strategies accordingly.

- **Revise the marketing plan for better results:** As you review your results during the year, you will find what is working well and what is not. Continuously adapt and evolve your marketing plan to reach new readers, sell more books, and maximize your success as an author.

Remember, in the ever-changing publishing landscape, creating an author marketing plan is an ongoing process. It requires your commitment to consistency, time, and budget to bring your marketing plan to life and then adapt to new strategies and opportunities.

How does a book launch differ from ongoing marketing?

A book launch and ongoing marketing efforts serve different purposes in an author's marketing strategy. For both traditionally and independently published authors, here are some key differences between a book launch and ongoing marketing efforts:

- **Goals:** The main goal of a book launch is to create buzz, generate immediate sales, and build momentum for a newly released book. If you are being traditionally published, the book launch is the biggest effort the publisher will provide to the author. For independently published authors, the entire process of the book launch falls on your shoulders. The goal of a book launch is to maximize initial visibility, securing positive reviews, and generating early reader engagement. Alternatively, the goal of ongoing marketing efforts is to maintain and expand the book's reach, nurture reader relationships, and drive consistent sales over an extended period.

- **Timing:** As you are getting ready to release a new book, the book launch is usually a few weeks to a couple of months of a focused marketing push. It involves concentrated promotional activities to generate excitement and drive initial sales. On the other hand, ongoing marketing efforts are aimed at sustaining interest, maintaining visibility, and growing a long-term readership.

- **Intensity and Scope**: A book launch is typically a highly focused and intense period of marketing activity to introduce the new book. During this time, authors often engage in a concentrated marketing push with activities like book signings, media interviews, guest blogging, and targeted advertising. After the initial launch, every author needs to continue ongoing marketing efforts. These are focused on maintaining visibility through regular content creation, social media engagement, email marketing, and periodic promotions to build book sales.

- **Budget Allocation**: Launching a new book usually requires more budget to create a big bang. A book launch often involves a higher budget amount compared to ongoing marketing efforts. If traditionally published, the company may provide an advance plus include costs to launch your book. Your book sales will first be used to earn back the investment by the publisher. Therefore, you may not see many royalties until those publisher costs are recovered. To gain more royalties, you, as the author, need to help promote book sales with your marketing plan.

Independently published authors must be prepared to fund all the publication costs. Funding is needed to invest in professional book cover design, editing, advertising, promotional events, and other launch-specific activities.

For <u>both</u> publishing routes, ongoing marketing efforts require a more sustainable and long-term budget allocation by you, the author. It involves consistent investment in activities like website maintenance, social media advertising, content creation, building an email list, and more.

- **Target Audience**: During a book launch, you are reaching out to prospective and target readers with content that excites their interest in your new book. The marketing efforts are tailored to create awareness among this specific audience segment. In ongoing marketing, the target audience may expand to include not only readers of the author's previous books but also new readers who may be interested in the author's genre.

- **Timeline:** A book launch has a clearly defined timeline, usually centered around the book's release date. It involves pre-launch activities, launch day promotions, and post-launch follow-ups. Ongoing marketing efforts are a continuous part of an author's overall marketing strategy and may be adjusted and refined as needed.

It is important to note that the excitement of a book launch can distract you from your ongoing marketing efforts. While it is an essential component of your marketing plan, your book launch must be supported by your commitment to strong marketing efforts for long-term book sales success. To build your author brand, grow readership, and sustain book sales, consistency and continued engagement with readers is critical beyond the initial launch period.

Author Brand

If I'm using a pseudonym or more than one, should I have everything on one website under my legal name or have separate websites for each name used?

Deciding whether to have one website with all your pseudonyms (pen names) or separate websites depends on several factors. Here are some considerations:

- **Author Branding**: Often having one consistent brand identity can be accomplished with a single website. While one website allows you to showcase all your books, series, and pen names, there can be confusion when pen names are used. For published authors, if a book or series has not sold well, a publisher may suggest new projects under a different name. Or, pen names are used for writing in a different genre. Here are two concepts:

  o For authors who publish under one name, devote the website to showcasing the book(s) and series. Have book covers as the main graphics on the home page.

  o For authors who use a pen name, focus your website content on you, the author, with a big headshot and bio on the home page.

- **Target Reader:** Consider whether your different pseudonyms cater to distinct target readers. If your pseudonyms cover diverse genres or writing styles that may not overlap, separate websites might be more appropriate. An example would be romance versus thriller, fantasy versus police procedural, or historical fiction versus nonfiction. Having a separate website allows you to create a focused online presence tailored to each pseudonym's audience.

- **Practicality:** Managing multiple websites can be time-consuming and require more effort in terms of content creation, maintenance, and marketing. If you prefer to streamline your online presence and consolidate your efforts, having a single website might be more practical.

- **Cross-Promotion**: If your pseudonyms are related or have some thematic connections, a single website can facilitate cross-promotion. It allows readers of one pseudonym to discover your other works, potentially increasing your overall readership.

- **Privacy and Separation**: If you wish to keep your pseudonyms completely separate for personal or privacy reasons, having separate websites can help maintain distinct online identities. This approach ensures that readers and industry professionals associate each pseudonym with its designated website. One example, a writer friend of mine had traditionally published thrillers and wanted to try her hand at steamy contemporary romance, so she began using a pen name. Her main website was all about her thrillers and only mentioned her romance pen name in her bio. Therefore, fans who visited the website would not find her romance titles to entice them to purchase one. A good solution would be a second website under the pen name to engage visitors about her ongoing romance series.

Ultimately, the choice between a single website or separate websites depends on your goals, target reader profile(s), time to manage multiple websites, and the budget you're willing to invest.

Pseudonyms/Pen Names in Social Media

For social media platforms, I have seen many authors use accounts with "author" at the end or as the pseudonyms they write under and wonder which to do?

Deciding whether to have one social media account or separate accounts for your author brand or each pen name depends on similar factors as the website question. Here are some considerations:

- **Branding:** The first issue is to have accounts using your author brand separate from your personal social media accounts. The initial author social media accounts help you establish a consistent author brand identity across all your social media. If you have pen names, having one author social media account can be beneficial to showcase your versatility.

- **Target Reader:** Consider whether your pseudonyms cater to distinct target reader audiences. The nod to having different social media accounts is important when genres differ significantly. Having separate social media accounts can help you tailor your content and engage directly with each pseudonym's readership.

- **Time and Effort**: Managing multiple social media accounts can be time-consuming. If you prefer to streamline your social media presence and consolidate your efforts, having one account can be more practical, especially if your pseudonyms overlap in terms of genre or writing style.

- **Cross-Promotion:** If your pen names are related or have some thematic connections, having one social media account can facilitate cross-promotion. It allows you to share updates, announcements, and promotions across all your pseudonyms, potentially reaching a wider audience.

- **Audience Expectations**: Consider the expectations of your readers and followers. Some may be interested in following all your pen names and prefer to see updates from all your writing endeavors in one place, while others may prefer to engage with a specific pen name.

It really boils down to the time you're willing to invest in managing multiple social media accounts. If you are fitting in your writing around a full-time job, consider streamlining with one author brand account on your social media platforms of choice. If you have more time or limit the number of social media platforms you consistently post on, the idea of having tailored accounts to promote your pen name(s) can be accomplished.

Email List & Messages

What are "best practices" for email marketing?

Email marketing is a direct way to connect with your readers because your e-newsletters and email promotions arrive in their inboxes. Different than social media that has an ongoing flow of posts that may be noticed or not, an email appears in their phone or laptop without other distractions. To make the most of your email marketing, here are some steps:

- **Choose an email marketing service**: Many of the reputable email marketing service providers have a free or low-cost option. The importance of these platforms is they offer tools to manage subscribers, create email campaigns, and track performance.to suit your needs. Popular options include Mailchimp, MailerLite and Constant Contact.

- **Create an opt-in form**: Design an opt-in form that captures email addresses from your website visitors. Place the form prominently on your website, preferably on the homepage or sidebar. Keep the form simple, requesting minimal information such as the reader's name and email address.

- **Offer freebies**: Provide something special to encourage visitors to subscribe to your email list. This can be in the form of a free e-book, exclusive content, a bonus chapter, or access to a reader community. The incentive should align with your book and appeal to your target readers.

- **Guest blogging and podcasts**: Find blogs to query for writing guest posts or appearing on a podcast of other authors or influencers in your genre. In your author bio, include a call-to-action to join your email list. This can help you reach new readers who are interested in your genre or niche.

- **Engage readers through your content**: Create valuable and engaging content through a blog, website, or social media platforms. Offer insights, writing tips, book recommendations, and behind-the-scenes glimpses into your writing process. Encourage readers to subscribe to your email list for more exclusive content and updates.

How do I continue to build an email list?

Building an email list is an effective way to connect with your readers directly and cultivate a dedicated audience for your books. Here are some steps to help you build an email list:

- **Use freebie offer with sign-up form**: Once you have the email sign-up form on your website, encourage visitors to subscribe with an incentive. It should be something special that aligns with your book and appeals to your target readers. You can then set it up to be emailed separately to the new subscriber. Or you can give a link to a form or PDF on your website for the new subscriber to download.

- **Promote your email list across platforms**: Promote your email list on various platforms to reach a wider audience. Share the link to your opt-in form on your website, blog, social media profiles, author bio, and author interviews. Mention the benefits of subscribing, such as receiving updates, exclusive content, and special offers.

- **Participate in book giveaways and promotions**: Collaborate with other authors or participate in book giveaways or promotions. Offer a free copy of your book in exchange for readers subscribing to your email list. Ensure that the giveaway or promotion reaches your target audience to attract interested readers.

- **Leverage author events and signings**: When attending book events, signings, or literary festivals, collect email addresses from interested readers. You can provide a sign-up sheet or use a tablet or smartphone to capture email addresses digitally. Make sure to inform readers that they'll receive updates and exclusive content by subscribing to your email list.

- **Comply with data protection regulations**: Ensure that you comply with data protection regulations such as the CAN-SPAM Act and the EU's General Data Protection Regulation (GDPR)[34] if applicable to your audience in foreign countries. Include a clear privacy policy and provide an option for subscribers to opt out or unsubscribe from your email list.

As building an email list takes time and consistent effort, be sure to focus on providing value to your target readers.

Social Media

What kind of schedule should I have for posting and why?

Having a consistent social media schedule to engage with target readers and promote your book(s) is a critical element in your marketing plan. Here's a sample schedule:

Daily Engagement:

- Briefly check each social media account and respond to comments, messages, and mentions promptly.

- Share interesting content from other authors, publishers, or literary resources.

- Like, comment, and share posts from followers and fellow authors.

Weekly Schedule:

- Monday: Share writing tips, advice, or motivational quotes to inspire.

- Tuesday: Feature a book review or recommend a book in your genre.

- Wednesday: Post book recommendations from your followers.

- Thursday: Share a short excerpt from your current work-in-progress.

- Friday: Offer to answer a question from readers about your writing process, characters, or upcoming projects.

- Saturday: Share a behind-the-scenes glimpse, such as your desk or favorite writing tools.

- Sunday: Take a break from promotional content and share something personal or non-writing related, like a hobby or a thought-provoking quote.

Monthly or Occasional:

- Host a contest to win a free signed copy of your book or other book-related prizes.

- Share finishing a manuscript, signing a publishing deal, or reaching a certain number of book sales.

- Collaborate with other authors for spotlights, joint giveaways, or cross-promotion of each other's work.

Remember it's also important to find a balance that helps you to be consistent.

What is an easy way to jumpstart and organize my social media content?

An easy "go-to" for posts is to set a calendar of holiday-themed content customized with your author brand and genre. Here is a list of national holidays and other key dates to get started:

- New Year's Day – January 1st

- Martin Luther King Jr. Day – 3rd Monday in January

- Groundhog Day – February 2nd

- Super Bowl Sunday– 2nd Sunday in February

- Valentine's Day – February 14th

- President's Day - 3rd Monday in February

- St. Patrick's Day – March 17th

- April Fool's Day – April 1st

- Easter – Changes each year in late March or early April

- Earth Day – April 22nd

- Mother's Day – 2nd Sunday of May

- Memorial Day – Last Monday in May

- Father's Day – 2nd Sunday of June

- Juneteenth National Independence Day - June 19th

- Independence Day – July 4th

- Labor Day – 1st Monday in September

- Columbus Day - 2nd Monday in October

- Halloween – October 31st

- Veteran's Day – November 11th

- Thanksgiving Day – 4th Thursday in November

- Black Friday – Day after Thanksgiving

- Cyber Monday – Monday after Thanksgiving

- Christmas – December 25th

- New Year's Eve – December 31st

- Just for Fun – Your Birthday (offer a special discount to celebrate?)

What promotion ideas to hook my target reader?

To jumpstart your creativity, consider these ideas with a holiday twist:

- **Checklists** – offer a free downloadable list of favorite books, your backlist, secret insights into your main characters. In essence, create a tangible and valuable tool your target reader will appreciate and remind them what perfect gifts your books can be.

- **Quiz** – develop a couple of questions about your story, your main characters, or something related to your genre (i.e. How to solve a mystery.) Relate a couple questions to how your character or genre may fit as a fun holiday gift.

- **Cheat Sheet** – build a list of fun facts about your characters, setting, or timeline. Your target reader will enjoy having some inside info. Plus, good time to remind them to give the cheat sheet with your book for a gift.

- **Video Message** – if you are comfortable making a video, you can provide a link to it on your YouTube channel or website. Add a little holiday flare in your background or an added holiday wishes at the end.

- **Podcast Episode** – when you are a guest on a podcast or if you have started one, use an embedded link to get target readers to hear from you, the author. Whether you talk about your book or series or decide to review some favorite authors who your target reader would enjoy, add a little holiday cheer to it.

- **Tokens** – many people enjoy collecting little tokens, often stickers or small items, for completing activities. For example, if you ask target readers some questions about your characters or story, then you can reward them with a token that can be redeemed for something on your website. Or use it as the "24 Days before Christmas" and offer tokens for completing different holiday inspired activities.

What tools can I use to make this easier?

There are many options in tools to help create content, especially for marketing projects. Here are a couple that are easy to use:

- Canva.com is a user-friendly graphic design tool that allows you to create stunning visuals for your social media posts. It offers a wide range of customizable templates, stock photos, fonts, and design elements, enabling you to create professional-looking graphics without the need for advanced design skills.

- HootSuite.com is social media management software that helps you create content and get more followers.

- Others include SproutSocial, BuzzSumo, and others that do have free trials and offer a variety of payment plans.

What about video for marketing?

Video can be a powerful tool because it enables you to connect with your target readers in a more personal and engaging way. Many authors are finding value in book trailers for their websites, shorts or reels in social media, and interviews uploaded to YouTube. Many authors film simple candid videos using a mobile phone, while others have a video-savvy person to help them. Still others, like me, use an easy-to-use video software program. The value of video according to The State of Video Marketing 2023 by Wyzowl found 96% of people surveyed have watched an explainer video to learn more about a product or service. Further, 89% of people say watching a video has convinced them to buy a product or service.[35]

Here are some ideas for incorporating videos into your social media schedule as an author:

- **Book Trailers:** Create short, visually appealing videos that provide a teaser or introduction to your book. Use music, imagery, and compelling text to capture viewers' attention and generate interest in your work.

- **Author Interviews**: Record video interviews where you discuss your writing journey, inspirations, and behind-the-scenes insights into your books. You can conduct these interviews yourself or collaborate with book bloggers, influencers, or fellow authors for a more interactive conversation.

- **Reading Excerpts:** Choose a captivating section from your book and record yourself reading it aloud. This allows your audience to experience your writing style and get a taste of your storytelling.

- **Writing Tips**: Share your expertise and provide valuable writing tips through short videos. Offer advice on plot development, character creation, or any other aspect of the writing process that you specialize in. These videos can be a great way to connect with aspiring writers and build your authority in the writing community.

- **Live Q&A Sessions**: Host live video sessions on platforms like Instagram Live, Facebook Live, or YouTube Live, where you can interact with your audience in real-time. Encourage viewers to ask questions about your books, writing process, or anything else they'd like to know.

- **Behind-the-Scenes Content**: Take your audience behind the scenes of your writing life. Show them your writing space, your favorite writing tools, or share snippets of your research process. These videos give your readers a glimpse into your world and help forge a stronger connection.

- **Alliances:** If you have other authors, book reviewers, or BookTok users who you know are willing to create joint videos. The best thing is that you can cross-promote by giving the other authors your video link content for their email list. Then, you can have the other authors send their video content to email to your list. The idea is you will have the potential to attract new subscribers. Topics can be about new releases, writing tips, books you're reading, reviews, or interviews.

Remember to optimize your videos for each social media platform you use. Use captions, engaging graphics or photos, and relevant hashtags (description in Chapter 6) to increase visibility and reach. And always encourage your viewers to share, comment, and engage with your content.

Final Thoughts

The strategies and ideas in this handbook are based on marketing fundamentals and designed to show you how to achieve your professional dreams and goals. These step-by-step methods, tips and tricks are meant to be fun while you create your marketing machine.

Hopefully, the information you have read in this handbook has inspired you to jump into marketing with the confidence to build your plan and enjoy putting promotions in place that enable you to engage with your target readers.

Your success as an author is often judged by how many books you sell. Putting an author brand marketing plan and budget together to promote your book(s) will help you reach higher sales levels and the success of your dreams.

BONUS:
The Ease of Using Artificial Intelligence (AI)

It is now much easier for you to "get words on the page" and create marketing material that is effective for you. AI language models such as ChatGTP/Open AI from Microsoft or other similar computer programs are fun to use for content, articles, blog posts, and art projects. The programs are trained to generate human-like responses, using "prompts" to produce the content you request. According to the website, **COSchedule.com,** "An AI Prompt is any form of text, question, information, or coding that communicates to AI what response you're looking for. Adjusting how you phrase your prompt; AI could provide varying responses."[36]

In fact, the better the prompt that you use to provide context for the AI software, the better and more specific the content it presents back to you. And it's ready in seconds!

There are AI tools offered by many websites and some are free, like ChatGPT, developed by OpenAI. The key is how to get the best results when you use them. Because an AI program does create content very quickly, it allows you to refine your prompt by adding more demographics of your target readers and help the content to really resonate with them.

Here are some tips:

- Try a prompt for what words to get a start on describing your target market. Here is an example:

  - o Q: "Who is the target reader for my amateur sleuth mystery that has a metaphysical twist with demographics?"

  - o A: Adults aged 25-55, both men and women, English speaking, with a high school education or above.

- Use AI to create your designs, email subject lines, social media posts and more to excite your target readers and sell your book(s). Here's an example:

Productivity Tip

Consider using an AI program as a Virtual Assistant. The good news is that it's **free** to help you get moving with your author brand and book marketing.

Log in to your AI program to:

- Ask for drafts of your marketing drafts, emails, social media posts and more.
- Request it to edit your writing projects.
- Have it answer questions to gather research for you.
- Design a book cover, ad or other graphic.

There are AI tools being used to create many more types of projects, even help you run your writing business.

o   Q: "What is a good email subject line for an amateur sleuth mystery with a metaphysical twist that a target reader aged 25-55 with a high school education, and female?"

o   A: **Uncover Mystical Secrets in Our New Amateur Sleuth Mystery**!

- When making a special offer, ask for some email copy. The example prompt below is one to get marketing copy which includes a discount amount as well as the name and who would enjoy it:

Q: "Generate email copy for a new book that is an amateur sleuth mystery with a metaphysical twist that a target reader aged 25-55 with a high school education, that is female and the book costs $9.99."

A: The following is the AI response with a book title, content, and without human editing:

Subject: Discover a Captivating Blend of Mystery and Metaphysics in Our New Release!

Dear [Reader's Name],

Are you ready to embark on an extraordinary journey that will challenge your intellect, ignite your imagination, and transport you into a world where mysteries intertwine with the metaphysical? We are thrilled to introduce our latest release, an amateur sleuth mystery with a mind-bending twist that will keep you on the edge of your seat.

*In **"Secrets Unveiled: The Enigmatic Chronicles,"** you will follow the enigmatic life of [Protagonist's Name], an ordinary individual who finds herself thrust into an extraordinary role as an amateur sleuth. As she navigates the puzzling world of detective work, a mysterious metaphysical twist adds an intriguing layer to her investigations.*

Prepare to unravel perplexing clues, immerse yourself in a web of secrets, and venture into realms beyond the ordinary. Our protagonist's unique abilities and uncanny intuition will challenge your perceptions of reality, as she delves into the hidden dimensions where the answers lie.

This captivating tale is tailored specifically for readers like you, aged 25-55, with a high school education and an insatiable thirst for both intellectual stimulation and thrilling entertainment. Whether you're a fan of mystery novels or have a deep fascination with metaphysical concepts, "Secrets Unveiled" promises to deliver an unforgettable reading experience that will leave you questioning the very fabric of existence.

To make it even more enticing, we're offering an exclusive launch price of just $9.99 for our valued readers. Grab your copy now and immerse yourself in a world where the ordinary merges with the extraordinary, and where the enigmatic becomes tangible.

*Don't miss out on this extraordinary opportunity to experience the amalgamation of mystery and metaphysics. Click the link below to order your copy of **"Secrets Unveiled: The Enigmatic Chronicles"** today!*

[CTA Button] Order Now

Join us on this riveting journey, as we unlock the secrets that lie beneath the surface and challenge the boundaries of conventional wisdom. Prepare to be enthralled, enlightened, and immersed in a gripping tale like no other.

Happy reading!

Best regards,

[Your Name]

Caution with Using AI

As a tool, AI is amazing for helping you develop content quickly and get past writer's block. Plus, the words generated pop up in seconds from your prompt. Yet, there are a few warnings that come with the use of AI.

- First, while a useful tool, it is not perfect. Please do not simply copy what the bot provides and use it for a post, article, or chapter. The bot is simply picking up content off the internet and you need to review, edit, and validate before using it for your projects.

- Second, the content found by the bot has been uploaded to the internet from other authors and copywriters. Therefore, you cannot copyright the document that uses content from these bot programs. There are plagiarism programs that will pick up blocks of copy that were not your original content.

- Finally, make sure to verify information within the AI response. For example, if there are mentions of facts, statistics, or quotes from famous people in the response, make sure to do Google searches to validate these. It is important to have cites to the web sites, books or studies that confirm the information is true. The AI bot is pulling content from the internet, so it might give you false or misleading info.

The best thing is to play with it! Go to ChatGPT and create a free account to try a variety of prompts for your marketing and writing.

ABOUT THE AUTHOR

Nicolette Lemmon, the innovative founder of LemmonTree Marketing Group, guided the marketing efforts of dozens of major corporations and financial institutions, designing award-winning campaigns to build name awareness and bottom lines. Many of her marketing solutions won coveted awards for her consulting firm and clients. She also developed and presented cutting edge seminars, training workshops, and key-note speeches to thousands of people in audiences from Puerto Rico to California, from Hawaii to New York and points in between with topics such as "Branding Concepts & Storytelling," "Jump Start Your Creative Batteries" and "Marketing Yourself for Future Success."

In addition, Nicolette wrote more than fifty articles for national and regional publications, as well as five non-fiction books, addressing strategies for business growth, target marketing, and other subjects to aid professionals in building business and profitability. Her popular book, ***Almost Famous: How to Market Yourself for Success***, helped people to achieve success in their careers and small businesses. Her weekly blog to inspire friends, ***Simply Stated Sundays***, (www.nicolettelemmon.com), has found fans and followers across the United States.

In writing her first fiction novel, Mind's Eye Murder, part of the "Reluctant Psychic Mystery" series, she was led to join the national organization, Sisters in Crime. Then, she helped found a local chapter, Grand Canyon Writers. Nicolette has served on the Board of Directors and developed a program entitled, The Mysteries & More Marketing Network. It was designed for both traditionally and independently published members for guidance in marketing themselves and to sell books. From this program, participants asked her for a handbook which led to creating this book as an easy-to-follow guide geared for writers who want to successfully sell their books in today's crowded marketplace.

Nicolette's additional qualifications include having earned a master's in business administration (MBA) from Arizona State University and she served on the faculty of five separate universities and institutes including for the University of Phoenix where she taught classes in marketing management. In addition to many prestigious marketing awards, she was nominated for Inc. Magazine's and Ernst and Young's, "Entrepreneur of the Year Award" in Arizona, received the "Top 100 Small Businesses-Arizona" award and "Top 50 Woman-Owned Businesses-Arizona" honors from DiversityBusiness.com for ten years.

Throughout her career, she volunteered for national and local charities in promoting their organizations to increase volunteer recruitment and donations. She has also served on the Board of Directors of Arizona Central Credit Union, a $750 million financial institution, since 2020.

For more information on Nicolette and her newest projects go to www.LemmonTree.com or www.nicolettelemmon.com.

Acknowledgements

A huge thank you to those people who helped me with insights, editing, and ideas for this handbook.

Dennis Koepke, my husband, and business partner spent time editing and discussing ideas that he applied from years of working with me at LemmonTree Marketing Group. His insights helped improve the descriptions of a variety of marketing terms.

Yvonne Corrigan Carr was a helpful editor and cheerleader who supported me with editing and suggestions. From her perspective as a writer, she helped make sure the handbook was easy to understand from both aspiring and published authors.

Cindy Ketcherside was kind to do a beta read and provided insights to improve the ease of using this handbook. She mentioned that having hired my firm to provide marketing solutions to her former company, the handbook was offering business insights that were understandable to authors who may never have had experience with marketing.

From the Sisters in Crime Grand Canyon Writers chapter, thanks to the group of authors that helped me develop and lead the Mysteries & More Marketing Network: Barbara Hinske, Erynn Crowley, Debra S, Sanders, and Charlotte Morganti. Their encouragement and that of the members who participated in the program led me to create this marketing handbook.

BIBLIOGRAPHY

1. Jack Canfield quote, https://www.aspiringwriteracademy.com/25-quotes-tips-and-advice-from-famous-authors/, page 1
2. 10 Awful Truths About Publishing, Berrett-Koehler Publishers, https://ideas.bkconnection.com/10-awful-truths-about-publishing, page 1
3. How Many Copies Do Most Fiction Books Sell, https://www.tagari.com/how-many-copies-do-most-fiction-books-sell/, page 1
4. There Are Now Over 12 Million Kindle Ebooks On Amazon, Just Publishing Advice, https://justpublishingadvice.com/there-are-now-over-5-million-kindle-ebooks/, page 2
5. Lewis Carroll quote, https://www.brainyquote.com/quotes/lewis_carroll_165865 , page 3
6. How I Made $1,928 Last Month Self-Publishing on Amazon, https://financequickfix.com/make-money-self-publishing-books-amazon/, page 3
7. Hank Phillippi Ryan, (https://hankphillippiryan.com/hank/), page11
8. Patricia Sargeant (aka Olivia Matthews, Regina Hart), (https://youtu.be/ivASYzGogfs), page 12
9. Mark Twain, https://www.azquotes.com/quote/399388, page 15
10. Seth Godin quote: https://quotefancy.com/quote/1208847/Seth-Godin-Everyone-is-not-your-customer, page 29
11. Wikipedia, https://en.wikipedia.org/wiki/Hashtag, page 40
12. Best-Hashtages.com, https://best-hashtags.com, page 40
13. Amazon Ads for Authors, (https://advertising.amazon.com/library/guides/basics-of-success-sponsored-ads), page 43
14. Ads for Authors, Mark Dawson, https://learn.selfpublishingformula.com/p/adsforauthors, page 42
15. Facebook and Instagram Ads for Authors, BookBaby, https://www.bookbaby.com/sell-your-book/facebook-ads-for-authors, page 43
16. USA Today Best-Selling and Award-Winning Author, Hank Phillippi Ryan, https://hankphillippiryan.com/, page 46
17. Raquel V. Reyes' tagline of "Latina Sleuths," https://rvreyes.com/, page 46
18. The 15 Biggest Social Media Sites and Apps [2023], https://www.dreamgrow.com/top-15-most-popular-social-networking-sites/#14_Pinterest_%E2%80%93_442_Million_Active_Users, page 47
19. Podcast Statistics and Data [March 2023], https://www.buzzsprout.com/blog/podcast-statistics, page 48
20. The infinite dial 2022, https://www.edisonresearch.com/the-infinite-dial-2022/, page 48
21. YouTube Hits a Billion Monthly Users, https://blog.youtube/news-and-events/onebillionstrong/ page 49
22. The infinite dial 2022, https://www.edisonresearch.com/the-infinite-dial-2022/,page 49
23. 20 Places to post your video not that its done, https://www.lemonlight.com/blog/20-places-to-post-your-video-now-that-its-done-1/, page 49

24. Glossophobia (Fear of Public Speaking): Are You Glossophobic? https://www.psycom.net/glossophobia-fear-of-public-speaking, page 53
25. How to overcome your fear of public speaking, https://www.britishcouncil.org/voices-magazine/how-overcome-fear-public-speaking, page 56
26. Tips for Maintaining Proper Dress Code For An Office, https://in.indeed.com/career-advice/starting-new-job/dress-code-for-office, page 56
27. The Importance of Eye Contact during a Presentation, https://virtualspeech.com/blog/importance-of-eye-contact-during-a-presentation#, page 57
28. Instagram Help Center, www.help.instagram.com, page 64
29. Facebook Help Center, www.facebook.com/help, page 64
30. Twitter Help Center, https://help.twitter.com/, page 64
31. YouTube (https://support.google.com/youtube/, page 64
32. You Now Have a Shorter Attention Span Than a Goldfish, https://time.com/3858309/attention-spans-goldfish/, page 66
33. Steve Martin quote, https://www.brainyquote.com/quotes/steve_martin_600008, page 77
34. 4 Things You Need to Know About Email Compliance, https://onesignal.com/blog/4-things-you-need-to-know-about-email-compliance/, page 88
35. The State of Video Marketing 2023, https://wyzowl.s3.eu-west-2.amazonaws.com/pdfs/Wyzowl-Video-Survey-2023.pdf, page 91
36. AI Prompt, https://coschedule.com/marketing-terms-definitions/ai-prompt, page 95

Notes:

Made in the USA
Middletown, DE
21 December 2023